Find Your Path *through* Depression

Mindful techniques for dark times

Quarto

First published in 2025 by Leaping Hare Press,
an imprint of The Quarto Group.
One Triptych Place
London, SE1 9SH,
United Kingdom
T (0)20 7700 9000
www.Quarto.com

Previously published as *Mindfulness for Black Dogs and Blue Days: Finding a Path Through Depression* in 2012.

Design Copyright © 2025 Quarto
Text Copyright © 2012, 2025 Richard Gilpin

Richard Gilpin has asserted his moral right to be identified as the Author of this Work in accordance with the Copyright Designs and Patents Act 1988.

All rights reserved. No part of this book may be reproduced or utilised in any form or by any means, electronic or mechanical, including photocopying, recording or by any information storage and retrieval system, without permission in writing from Leaping Hare Press.

Every effort has been made to trace the copyright holders of material quoted in this book. If application is made in writing to the publisher, any omissions will be included in future editions.

A catalogue record for this book is available from the British Library.

ISBN 978-0-7112-9856-9
Ebook ISBN 978-0-7112-9857-6

10 9 8 7 6 5 4 3 2 1

Text designed and typeset by Dinah Drazin

Editorial Director: Monica Perdoni
Commissioning Editor: Sophie Lazar
Editor: Katerina Menhennet
Senior Designer: Renata Latipova
Production Controller: Rohana Yusof

Printed in the UK

The information in this book is for informational purposes only and should not be treated as a substitute for professional counselling, medical advice or any medication or other treatment prescribed by a medical practitioner; always consult a medical professional. Any use of the information in this book is at the reader's discretion and risk. The author and publisher make no representations or warranties with respect to the accuracy, completeness, or fitness for a particular purpose of the contents of this book and exclude all liability to the extent permitted by law for any errors and omissions and for any injury, loss, damage, or expense suffered by anyone arising out of the use, or misuse, of the information in this book, or any failure to take professional medical advice.

Find Your Path *through* Depression

Mindful techniques for dark times

Richard Gilpin

Leaping Hare Press

Contents

Introduction 7

CHAPTER ONE
Dark Times, Dead Ends & Breakdowns 13

CHAPTER TWO
Finding a Foothold, Clearing a Path 41

CHAPTER THREE
Fresh Prints on an Old Trail 71

CHAPTER FOUR
Hello Darkness, My Old Friend 101

CHAPTER FIVE
Signposts for the Way Ahead 123

Endnotes 138
Index 141
Acknowledgements 143
About the Author 144

Introduction

This book is about just two things: mindfulness and depression. Both are concepts that refer to particular psychological states or processes, but because these states are experiences, neither is particularly easy to encapsulate in language. Such is the nature of the seamless yet transient flow of moments that constitute our existence, we can't ever fully capture them with words. That's OK, because to cultivate a mindful path out of depression ultimately means going beyond words and towards the freedom of clear, unelaborated awareness. This is something we must do in our own way; but I hope the pointers in this book might help you along.

Just as the most unassuming situations hold the potential for wisdom and profound connection, they might equally give rise to ignorance and entanglement. When I think about the concepts of mindfulness and depression, I think of two stories – one historical and one personal – both of which take place in a bathtub.

Bathing in the Light of Wisdom

Do you know the (true) story of Archimedes in the bath? Archimedes, a renowned scholar in ancient Greece, had been asked to determine whether his king's new gold wreath was made purely of gold or whether some silver had been substituted by a dishonest goldsmith. It was proving an intractable problem, particularly as Archimedes could not reshape, melt down or in any way tamper with the precious crown. Disconcerted, he decided to suspend his mental exertions for the day and take a bath.

As he immersed himself in the water, he noticed that the level in the tub rose as his body descended. In that moment, it dawned on him that this effect was produced by the amount of water displaced by his submerged body. There followed another realization for him: this effect could be used to determine the volume of the gold wreath by submerging *it* in water! Already knowing its weight, he would then be able to calculate its density, or mass per unit volume, and compare this to the same weight of pure gold coins. If the two results were different, the wreath was not made of pure gold; if they were the same, it was.

Eureka!

Archimedes had found the answer to his problem. Not a bad day's work after all. The tale goes that, in his excitement, he exclaimed 'Eureka!' ('I've found it!'), leapt from the bath and ran naked through the streets.

Putting aside Archimedes' discovery of how to determine the volume of an object with an irregular shape, not to mention his impulsive streak in public, there is something very interesting about this story. It concerns the moment, or moments, prior to his discovery. Consider that Archimedes had given up his mathematical problem-solving when he took to the water. He wasn't pondering on precious metals, royal headgear or scientific experiments. In fact, he wasn't in 'thinking mode' at all. He was easing himself into a relaxing tub and absorbed in his sensory experience, just as any of us might be when slipping into a bath after a hard day.

His attention was, in those crucial moments, with his immediate experience in such a way that it allowed him to see clearly, to be fully present to *what was occurring*: water rising before his eyes. This facilitated a moment of insight – the natural capacity we each have for uncovering truth.

A Hallmark of Mindfulness

You've probably had these 'aha' moments yourself – a dawning of some knowledge that seems to happen *to* you *and* within you. Like those times where you might hear yourself saying something deeply sensible or profound to someone, only to muse afterwards, 'Where did *that* come from? I didn't know I knew that!' It's as if you somehow managed to 'get out of the way' and allowed something wonderful to emerge. This can happen for any of us when we relax into our present experience and allow space for what is occurring. It is this 'way of being' that is one of the hallmarks of mindfulness.

Cold Water Blues

One otherwise average day, sitting in a bath, I too had a memorable experience. It conveyed a powerful message about my state of being at the time. It captures nothing of what I know about mindfulness, but much of what I know about depression.

I was home alone, freshly scrubbed in the water, the dim afternoon light permeating the bathroom curtains. The day had been a forgettable blur of tasks, nothing too taxing. Yet I could not shake off a sense of disconsolation. I splashed at the tepid water with my hand, trying to retrieve something tangible from the recent past. My mind began inclining uneasily towards the future, recasting it into ever darker shapes. Half-formed and unanswerable questions like 'What now?' and 'What next?' began orbiting each other in repetitive cycles. Soon I could no longer discern any interest or potential comfort in the days ahead. Nor any value to the past or present. My mood went into freefall. My body fell as still as the water.

The Face in the Depths
Later, bath long gone cold, a sudden downward motion roused me. It was my head falling forwards, as if unable to bear its own weight. My eyes momentarily focused on their own reflection.

I took a long look at my own face. There I was, down under the grey water, behind the dead skin cells and grime of the day, submerged and unreachable, staring back at myself with hollow, loveless eyes.

Who is that cold, hard starer? The part of me that's dead? The part of me that kills himself? The questions kept coming and my mood kept tumbling. My heart felt as if it was breaking at the edges. Rather than face the day, I faced this starer and he saw me all the way, dragging me further into darkness. All desire to move my life in a fresh direction waned as we battled to a predictable stalemate.

Me and my stale mate indeed. I know him well. Sometimes, for days at a time, we have become frozen in each other's gaze, stuck in an unwinnable face-off, disconnected from any decent sense of living while the world turns around us. It's a relationship with my inner world that is as futile as it is familiar and as deadening as it is comfortable. Psychologically speaking, it is a relationship to life that has the gravitational pull of a black hole. It conveys something to me of this thing called depression.

Cleaning Up & Moving On

I eventually got out of that bath. And other dead zones like it. As someone who has suffered depression and knows its recurring tendencies, I'm interested in learning the art of getting out of these places with greater ease, even style sometimes. As a practising therapist, who works with people suffering with depression, I'm also interested in what helps each of us loosen ourselves from its unsympathetic grip. The key has to do with acknowledging, even honouring, what we are struggling with and finding ways to be on better terms with it.

That's what this book is about – the continuing practice of getting out of the cold and ensnaring places of life, with an acceptance that these places do exist and are a part of our lives. It's also about understanding the relationship between Archimedes' bath-time experience and mine – and how we can have more of his and less of mine.

Just as there are different ways of taking baths, there are different ways of living lives. Regardless of how dark and downbeat the places you may find yourself, there always exists the potential of another path, one seasoned by the ordinary yet transformative quality of mindfulness. This path has led me out of many cold spots and likely will again. As with walking any path, the skill is in finding it and following it. And it's the journey, not the destination, that really matters.

CHAPTER ONE

Dark Times, Dead Ends & Breakdowns

Depression is not one thing. It is a coalescence of states of the body, heart and mind. Our experience of depression is subjective and, therefore, unique. Getting to know our depression – its colours and shades, its textures and tones – is the basis for understanding and resolving it. To create a map of its territory enables us to navigate it more effectively. We can do this with the help of others who have gone before us. For since the dawn of time, human beings have found themselves lost in depression's trackless wastes and have lived to tell their tales.

Life in the Shadows

Just as all things in this world of form and substance cast a shadow, the experience of living has its dark side. Happiness, joy and love must coexist with sadness, humiliation and aversion. And so it is that depression, with all its shapes and signatures, is just one of the necessary expressions of human existence.

I once quizzed a psychotherapist for a definition of depression and all she said was 'Rodin's *Thinker*', before lowering her head and resting her chin on the back of one hand to imitate the famous Parisian's early twentieth-century bronze and marble sculpture. I felt short-changed. I'd been hoping for a sophisticated clinical description that shed light on something I had experienced but had little objective knowledge of. Years later, I came to appreciate her response.

By then, I had come to notice how this bodily posture was modelled everywhere, from classical art pieces like Dürer's *Melencolia I* and Van Gogh's *At Eternity's Gate* to government-sponsored posters for 'depression awareness' campaigns. More importantly, I had also observed how the real, live, struggling people I knew would appear to physically sag in front of me.

To hold one's head in one's hands truly is the embodiment of depression. Try it for yourself and notice how it affects your mood. Notice how the inspiration of breath becomes effortful, how gravity drags on your body. Notice how your mental frame of reference narrows. Consider how your energy would congeal if you stayed like this for any length of time. States of depression are deeply connected to this sense of weight and contraction in the body. They give rise to a kind of stasis as the inner life grinds to a cheerless halt.

Weight of Being

Depression literally means 'being forced downward'. It is, therefore, a state of emotional heaviness and a movement within us, one where our vital energy is painfully compressed. Our very sense of aliveness is suffocated by the internal depths to which we plummet.

Stress results, and the discomfort can take many forms. Emotions of sadness, anxiety, anger, envy, guilt and shame mingle uneasily with notions of helplessness and worthlessness. Despite this apparently rich cocktail of negativity, the dulling of awareness that accompanies depression stifles our capacity to feel, frequently to the point of anhedonia: the inability to experience any pleasure.

Thus, it is understandable that motivation dwindles and apathy, disinterest and aversion to activity take over. Withdrawal from normal everyday behaviour, social contact and pastimes that were once enjoyable is commonplace for sufferers. Some people lose their appetite for food, others overeat. Moderation of the most basic human functions can become challenging. Sleeping problems, restlessness, difficulties concentrating and physical health problems often arise.

> She left the room undusted, did not care
> To hang a picture, even lay a book
> On the small table. All her pain was there –
> In absences. The furious window shook
> With violent storms she had no power to share.
>
> FROM 'A DEPRESSION', COLLECTED POEMS
> Elizabeth Jennings[1]

Hitting the Blocks

The depressed mind customarily takes to brooding. Its contents stray and collide in a vacuum of hope. Depression is not one 'thing', rather a syndrome of dis-ease with oneself and one's world. Given that life is continually rubbing up against the future, depression becomes a repeatedly failing attempt to flee our very existence.

The first time I recall 'depressing' was in my twenties. I had returned to my native home after a long voyage of (what I had thought was) self-discovery – travelling across continents by bus, bike and mule, and living out all my dreams of adventure in wild places. But I had found my dreams to be wanting. There had been no lasting earthly paradise to be found; there had been no transcendence beyond the unwanted aspects of life, such as loneliness, ageing and working for a living.

One winter's afternoon, housebound on a wet, Irish hilltop, buried in my own cyclical thinking, I lay face down on my bed and simply couldn't get up. Feelings of being at odds with the universe and weighed down by an impending future only served to amplify the critical thoughts and rumbling sadness.

A view of myself and my world, both inner and outer, as somehow defective quietly formed at the edges of my mind. That bed became my refuge from a perceived life of futility. Any sense of my physical environment receded as my attention narrowed inwards and downwards, intoxicated by a strange blend of disdain and conceit. I stopped eating and stayed put for two, maybe three days. Sadness enveloped me but no tears came. In order to feel anything, I occasionally punched the walls, breaking the skin on my knuckles just enough to confirm that I was still alive.

Lost in Space

The Romantic composer Hector Berlioz articulated his own depression as a terror characterized by 'the dreadful sense of being alone in an empty universe, the agonies that thrilled through me as if the blood were running ice-cold in my veins, the disgust with living, the impossibility of dying'.[2]

He also speaks of being tortured by a crushing sense of absence and isolation. Not all depressions deliver such extensive existential pain but his description points towards their commonly immobilizing impact. My own experiences are all linked to a sense of being 'stuck', whether that be outwardly, to a bed or a bathtub, or inwardly, to despairing thoughts that deliver nothing but greater blows to my morale.

On that wet, Irish hilltop, as I failed to get to grips with what was happening to me, I felt as though I were balancing on the

> Midway upon the journey of our life, I found myself within a forest dark, for the straightforward pathway had been lost.
>
> FROM 'INFERNO', DIVINE COMEDY
> Dante Alighieri, 1265–1321[3]

rim of a vast tank of liquid despair, desperate not to fall in yet unable to break free. All I could do was shuffle around the rim, at times successfully forgetting my situation, only to slip and plunge the moment I paused to consider it. Soon I grew tired of the fruitless circling and began entertaining suicidal fantasies of a fateful collapse and descent to the cold, grey bottom, never to return.

I managed to grant myself a reprieve from such finalities and scrape my way out of that tank, dripping in my own misery, exhausted at the balancing act I felt compelled to perform.

The Hour of Lead

This sense of imprisonment reflects the vision of medieval and Renaissance scholars, who considered the depressed person to be 'a child of Saturn', a planet traditionally seen as cold and distant and symbolized as a reaper or an old man who presided over the good old days, all now gone.[4] When we are 'in Saturn', we are fastened to a view of there being no future. Qualities of weight permeate the analogies with this planet, where the past hangs as heavy as lead, its alchemical metal. The poet Emily

Dickinson likened depression to the 'hour of lead',[5] again capturing a sense of its density and dullness.

Snapshots of Depression

There is a growing awareness of the prevalence of depression. The World Health Organization predicts that this century it will be the world's most disabling condition, above cancer and AIDS. Statistics suggest one in five people will experience depression at some point in their lives. It is also an illness that underscores other mental disorders and can have a devastating impact on physical health, relationships and finances.

This may be shocking but should not suggest the phenomenon is new. It is just better understood now. Depression has plagued human hearts and minds throughout history, including many of its most influential and creative members. Compiling alphabets of famous depressives is a cinch. Take, for example, European men. Start with Alexander the Great, proceed to Baudelaire, and on to Camus, Darwin, Elgar, Freud, Gauguin, Handel… and keep going. You might hit a blank at 'x', such is its limited application for most European names, but you can always pick up again with Émile Zola. To be depressed is to be in distinguished company.

As Old as Methuselah

You can scan the world's religious texts for further evidence that depression has been around since records began. Take the Bible for instance. King Solomon is regularly cited as a sufferer.

> Over them only was spread an heavy night, an image of that darkness which should afterward receive them: but yet were they unto themselves more grievous than the darkness... Then suddenly visions of horrible dreams troubled them sore, and terrors came upon them unlooked for.
>
> FROM 'WISDOM OF SOLOMON',
> 17:21 & 18:17 [6]

Others include Abraham, Jonah, Elijah, King Saul and Jeremiah. One of the most prominent accounts of depression is that of Job, whose suffering at the hand of God, to test Job's righteousness, leads to his descent into hopelessness, despondency and irritability. As far back as we can go, depression has been a travelling companion on the human journey.

Symbols of Melancholy

The traditional word for depression was melancholia, a collective term for a variety of complaints from sadness and lethargy to existential fear and dementia. Melancholia was seen as much as a physical condition as a significant cluster of what we now refer to as mental disorders.

Hippocrates, the greek physician, believed melancholia to be a disturbance of the body humours, notably black bile. Qualities of blackness figure heavily in representations of depression, as do deep shades of grey and blue – colours of the night and the cold. Traditional imagery also emphasizes depression's clinging nature and proximity. Its forms may shift but its presence lingers like a shadow.

The affliction's best-known metaphor is the 'black dog', which conjures up images of a threatening, unpredictable companion. 'The black dog is on his back' is old English slang employed for a dispirited or moody person. Amid my native Irish hills, the folks talk of 'wrestling with the black dog'. The unwanted company of the beast is apparent in both. Possession by a menacing creature is also suggestive of a superstition that black dogs were harbingers of doom. To host such a demonic presence tallied with an earlier view that melancholia came about through the devil's influence.

Despite its varied usage, 'black dog' as a specific term for depression only became popular through its adoption by the former British Prime Minister Winston Churchill (1874 –1965) to denote his gloomy moods. The expression is now here to stay, utilized by nationwide campaigns for tackling depression and enlisted by artists and thinkers for its sense of raw and ghostly power. You only need listen to the haunting song *Black-Eyed Dog* by Nick Drake, a tragic sufferer, for a sense of the animal's influence on a delicate human mind.

IDENTIFYING YOUR DARK COMPANION

Finding an image, or images, that symbolize your depression is a useful exercise for working skilfully to overcome it. Take time to contemplate the thoughts and feelings you associate with your darkest times.

What comes to mind when you think of depression? What colours, sounds and textures do you associate with it? Tune into the atmosphere of your mind. Allow images or metaphors to emerge, gently prompted by your enquiry. Resist any urge to rationalize, explain or interpret. What arises does not have to 'make sense' to anyone else. It only has to convey your experience.

This draws upon your innate creativity and, more importantly, provides some information that will allow you to begin developing a different kind of relationship with depression – one of enhanced recognition and greater objectivity.

Getting to know your depression in different ways lies at the heart of a mindful approach to it. You don't have to like it but you do have to know it. If you can develop a more acute sense of when depression is 'on your back' (or, even better, about to spring), then you will be better placed to deal with it.

Unconscious Abodes

You can mine the imagery of your depression by consulting your dreams. The value and significance of the unconscious has long been understood in spiritual tradition and psychotherapy. Typical dreams of the depressed are well documented, such as the dreamer portrayed as inept or defective and his goals thwarted. Settings might be a cave, cellar, seabed or sewer – representations of exile in the undersides of the world and navigation of places that are foreign and oppressive.

Night-time settings and black colours in dreams suggest isolation or termination of life. Winter conditions may also feature, indicating the emotional weather systems active in your waking life. Animals you feel uneasy around may present themselves. Archetypal creatures (the devil, the martyr) may put in an appearance. Be curious about your dream life. What backdrops and characters does your depression like to inhabit?

Dream Dogs

In those dark months in wintry Ireland, I had numerous nightmares, two of which involved a black dog that would prowl past me and then disappear. The one that remains vivid to this day is where I am standing in the dusky hallway of my grandmother's house, a place that always scared me as a child. A repugnant ball of meat hangs by a cord from the ceiling. The air is stale, motionless. Then I jolt backwards as a dog, sleek and strong, bolts from a doorway across the hallway and then vanishes before me.

> Depression is essential to the tragic sense of life.
> It moistens the dry soul, and dries the wet. It brings refuge,
> limitation, focus, gravity, weight, and humble powerlessness.
> It reminds of death. The true revolution begins in the
> individual who can be true to his or her depression.
>
> FROM 'A BLUE FIRE'
> James Hillman[7]

I remain curious about my black dog encounters because I was not aware of dreaming about such animals before. I doubt I knew anything of the metaphorical link with depression. I certainly had no idea that black dream dogs are often interpreted as representing death or impending bad weather. Judging by brief journal notes I kept at the time, this would have made good sense to me.

Journey into a Black Hole

Black holes are the densest singular objects in the known universe and are caused by a star collapsing in upon itself. They exert so much gravitational force that nothing can escape them, not even light. They are also invisible – and the best-fit metaphor for my own depression.

> Nothing escapes.
> The death of a man
> and his soul
> is the sound,
> the cosmic jester laughing,
> of life in the maw
> of merciless gravity,
> the swirling oblivion
> of Beelzebub's black hole.
>
> 'BLACK HOLE'
> William Hammett[8]

If you were able to watch someone fall into a black hole, you wouldn't notice anything other than that they would seem to slow down the nearer they got to the 'event horizon', the imperceptible point at which the gravitational pull becomes so immense that avoidance or escape becomes impossible. The person would then simply fade from view – you would not see where they went or how they disappeared. This is also true if you were to journey into a black hole yourself. You would not know at what point you had crossed the event horizon, but soon you would feel the tugging and pulling of colossal gravity.

I often experience a sense of closing down and entrapment with depression. It's as if a dimmer switch on my life is being turned down. As the lights drop low I cannot see clearly.

What were once refined objects become amorphous shapes that glint with veiled hostility. I feel disconnected with what is around me. Invisible barriers erect themselves between what I define as 'me' and what I define as 'not me'. This separation stifles communication. Choices and possibilities for action shrink as I grow quiet and slip undetectably into a retreat from contact. I occupy a place of great internal pressure and become trapped in it and by it.

While I feel victimized by this whole process (and my thoughts often reflect this), I also become deeply angry at my own complicity with it. Confined in a prison of my own making leaves me feeling even more hopeless and useless. And so the depressive snare tightens.

White Holes & Wormholes

Scientific theory suggests that once you're in a black hole, you're in it for good, due to the incredible crush of gravity. But what would actually *happen* if you passed into one still baffles science's greatest minds. The centre of the hole is known as a 'singularity', a dimensionless point of infinite density where the laws of physics break down. Here, space and time cease to exist in any meaningful way. They become irrelevant. It is so theorized that time travel, or travel to different universes via so-called 'wormholes', could be possible. Or that you could get spewed out the other side of a black hole via its polar opposite – a 'white hole'.

The magnetic pull into a depressed state and the subsequent languishing there routinely feels like there is no other possible dwelling to be had and the only future on the cards is more of the same. Yet past experience tells me different. I *do* find a way out. Whether it's by wormhole, white hole, blowhole or trap door doesn't matter. Getting out is what matters (and hopefully learning something worthwhile in the process). Subsequent chapters in this book are dedicated to skilful disengagement from depressed states.

Nothing Lasts for Ever
The most important thing to keep in mind is the illusion of the permanency of all psychological black holes. Nothing lasts for ever. Trusting that you can take something useful from your experiences down there will also grow with experience. I have come to be inspired by the idea that radical transformation, often via inexplicable means, can be found in the heart of our deepest suffering, just as great mystery and wondrous possibilities lie at the centre of a black hole.

Depression in a Different Light

Many ancient traditions understood the importance of recognizing the dark and denied aspects of our mind. As the famous inscription at the Temple of Apollo reads, 'Know thyself'. In so doing, we achieve a greater sense of wholeness. In this regard, depression can be a contributor of rare and precious knowledge.

> What is it, then, O mortal man,
> that has thrown you down into the slough of
> grief and despondency? You must have seen something
> strange and unexpected. But you are wrong if you think
> Fortune has changed towards you. Change is her normal
> behaviour, her true nature.
>
> FROM 'THE CONSOLATION OF PHILOSOPHY'
> Boethius, 480–524 AD[9]

The intensity, confusion as well as disorientation of some depressions can leave us feeling like life is falling apart. Previously stable, balanced views of self, world and future become redundant in the face of emotional upheaval. Old certainties we have been clinging to are swept aside. What is uncovered appears as a bottomless darkness, prompting a questioning of life at its deepest level. Depression, at such times, is a manifestation of an existential crisis.

Such crises are described and addressed by many of the world's psychological and spiritual traditions as an encounter with the mysteries of being, one that offers the potential for profound growth and renewal. This was memorably captured by a sixteenth-century Spanish mystic, Saint John of the Cross, in his poem *Dark Night of the Soul*. This poem recounts his inner journey from a place of darkness – 'without a light to guide, except the heart that lit me from inside'[10] – towards one of illumination and peace.

Buried Treasure

Dark nights of the soul are not ailments to be removed or overcome, but are an acknowledgement that 'progress' through life is not necessarily linear, consciously directed or, at times, even possible. Sometimes we need to retreat to deeper spaces within us in order to process the pain of our existence. Sometimes we need to listen to the darkness in our hearts. In doing so, we can discover new resources in ourselves and become enriched as a result. The journey through a dark night takes courage and fortitude.

It is for each of us to discover the importance of listening to our depression and granting it permission to speak the primal language of a dark night. At the very least, to discover that depression has meaning and value, rather than their absence, is soothing. This puts us back into contact with what really matters in life.

Spanners in the Works

Depression has energy. Its impact may be deadening and insinuate a seizing up/shutting down of our psycho-physical functioning. Our 'felt' experience may be an absence of any personal agency. But feelings are not reliable guides when we are in the grip of disorienting inner gloom.

Feelings can feed a broader misapprehension of what it is that's happening in the depths of our mind and heart. The sense of disconnection from our normal way of being, and our tirelessly negative evaluations of living, do not arise in a vacuum. So what is happening, dynamically, within us during a period of depression?

In recent years, neuroscientific researchers have been examining depression from an evolutionary viewpoint. Human brains, like those of other animals, are hard-wired to deal with threats and seek safety via innate emotional and behavioural responses. We have, in effect, inbuilt protective mechanisms.

If confronted by something hostile, we will automatically feel a certain way (angry, anxious or fearful) and act accordingly (fight, flee, freeze or submit). Much evidence suggests that these automatic defence systems are activated in depression, with associated changes in our brain state patterns precipitating 'threat emotions' like anxiety, irritability and dread. Far from shutting down, the brain is actually 'firing up'.

Animal Instincts

The evolutionary function of this automatic process makes sense when you consider the conditions under which it might be useful for us to inhibit ourselves and be more negative. Loss of close attachments, helplessness and entrapment in regard to life stressors, social isolation, conflict and defeat are some of the conditions that trigger depression-related brain state patterns.[11] If we feel we have no hope of success, no possibilities for control or escape, then of course we go into 'shut down'.

Seen in this light, depression is an adaptive response to a perception that what we have done (or experienced) will only lead to greater loss, frustration and failure. Psychologist and writer Paul Gilbert summarizes this age-old human behaviour as the drive to 'go to the back of the cave and stay there until things improve'.[12]

Depression's 'useful' role in our life is, alas, only one part of a bigger picture. As you may intuitively know, depression can easily flip into being dysfunctional. It all depends on how we relate to the events or situations that give rise to it. Can we accept what has happened, come to terms with what we have lost, and then move on? Or do we consider what has happened as a failure or rejection of 'me as a person' and go into a state of inner conflict? What we 'do', psychologically speaking, at such times is crucial in determining whether we move out of depression or reinforce it.

Can't Think Straight

The defensive reactions of the primitive brain affect how we think. In threat mode, our attention narrows, as do our appraisals of the world around us. Life is perceived as a much more confined and scary concern. The urge to flee is understandable – but how can you escape from your own mind?

> Melancholy drives us to where we can
> think and imagine no further, to the inmost void which is also
> the furthest limits of the mind.
>
> FROM 'A BLUE FIRE'
> James Hillman[13]

In depression, our normally agile thinking processes constrict to produce a sludge of negative generalizations about self and situation, all smattered with an array of exaggerated, biased and overly dramatic perceptions: 'It's all my fault… this is a total disaster… I'm inept at everything… everybody hates me… it's so unfair… it's always been like this… it always will be… it's all my fault…'

Pessimism and self-denigration are the motifs of this mindset. Memories of all the times things didn't work out are recalled relatively easily. Compelling notions that life is intolerable, that we are somehow defective, and powerless to adapt or change, flood the thinking mind. The emotional impact is, inevitably, an absence of all feelings of positivity and ease with oneself. Often our anger and disappointment are directed against ourselves in the form of self-critical thinking.

The whole grisly show, where each line of the script backs up all the others, is rather mesmerizing for a mind so depleted that it can only absorb confirmation of its own distorted logic. We become lost in its Kafkaesque labyrinth of adverse twists and obstructions, where Kafka himself could have drafted the cardinal article of faith: 'There is hope, but not for us.'[14]

Stuck in the Cud

The negative content of thinking is intrinsic to depression. The perpetual dwelling on this content – a mental activity called rumination – is even more important to understand. It is what keeps us bound to our gloom. The word 'rumination' comes from the Latin *ruminare*, meaning 'to chew over again'. Mammals such as cattle, sheep and goats are ruminators because they don't eat and digest food once but instead re-chew the cud to stimulate digestion.

There is no such benefit to the mental rumination of depressed humans. Dwelling on our difficulties, losses, failures and miserable prospects has debilitating emotional and behavioural consequences. It also leads to further brooding on why we feel so bad. Our mind gets caught in a loop, seduced by the idea that ruminating will solve our problems when all it does is generate more distasteful cud to chew on.

How to Do Your Own Head In

Depression can lead to a generalized emotional deadness. By attempting to escape from the negative feelings we are experiencing, we become cut off from all emotions, pleasant and unpleasant. What happens when our emotions are denied expression? They don't just vanish, that's for sure. We are feeling creatures and feelings will out! Physical problems, such as those with sleep and concentration, may result, as can various psychological symptoms when the mind tires in its efforts to suppress.

A special mention must go to anger, which can play a major role in depression when it bubbles away unacknowledged. When we direct anger (which comes in many forms, from disappointment and resignation to full-blown rage) at ourselves, the result is a loss of self-esteem and feelings of inadequacy. It is like taking a stick to oneself, where the ongoing barrage of self-criticism leaves us beaten and bruised. Taken to its extreme, anger turned against the self becomes suicide: 'Murder in the 180th degree', as Sigmund Freud put it.

For me, one of the faces of depression is that of the silent assassin, who steals quietly around my mind, seeking to kill. While he is busy shooting me up from the inside, I'm playing hard and quiet on the outside, holding back from authentic contact with the world. When he is active, I often appear the opposite, as if I 'can't be bothered'. Inwardly, I'm burrowing further into states of isolation and rejection.

Understanding that depression can be driven by turning feelings against ourselves suggests that depression is, psychodynamically speaking, something we 'do'. This implies that if we are willing to clarify, address and take responsibility for what's happening, we can choose to 'not do' depression.

Sources of Suffering

Just as every human being is unique, every human being's depression is unique. From the mild to the severe, the momentary to the long-lasting, depressions come in many forms. Like the weather, they arise based upon the prevailing conditions.

In Britain, where I live, TV news often makes reference to depressions – the ones that are systems of low atmospheric pressure responsible for much of our changeable weather. Their conditions are numerous, such as temperature, direction and speed of air currents. They produce cloudy, rainy and windy weather. We have a good sense of how they work, but that doesn't make them predictable or identical to each other. This is similarly the case for human depression.

Each of us is a product of causes and conditions. For starters, our parents (who are also products of theirs). Next, our nurturing and our early experiences of human life. Then, everything that happens to us and in us throughout life. Plus, all our responses to all of that! So, how we come to be who we are is a subtle and complex process, which is ongoing. Difficulties and disturbances with our mood state are one part of this process. Depression can arise mainly from environmental factors (including life events such as the loss of a loved one), biological predisposition, or both. It can be occasional or chronic, cyclical or apparently random. To explore and learn about the conditions that give rise to your depression, without wallowing in them, is a delicate balancing act.

Grinding to a Halt

When I reflect on those bleak days, bed-bound, on a cold Irish hill, I can look from a perspective that was not available then. I had invested heavily (emotionally and financially) in a one-way ticket to exotic adventure, only to discover that resources are finite and wanderlust fades. My anticipation of more and better stimulation/joy/fun, which had been continually re-imagined as I moved from mountain to desert, beach to city and continent to continent, had crumbled to dust.

As time rolled on, I had become hooked on the rides between these places because the places themselves failed to deliver the novelty I sought. Then, at the tail-end of the trip, I had fallen into a relationship with a woman travelling in the opposite direction to me. She was now thousands of miles away and I had little hope of seeing her again. I had a galling sense that my life was hell-bent on going the wrong way.

What hurt even more was the realization that the story I had told myself (and others) before going travelling – namely that I was solely driven by a quest for new horizons, mystery and action – was only partly true. My urge to wander was as equally inspired by my wish to flee displeasing aspects of my life. Some of these were external conditions, such as unsatisfactory work and social life, and some were internal, such as troublesome anxiety and low self-esteem. The former I was now confronting again; the latter I had never escaped from, merely carried around as psychic baggage. It dawned on me that I had, to a large extent, run away, and now I found myself 'returned to sender' with no prospects for a fresh delivery elsewhere. To a self-styled (and self-absorbed) traveller, there was no sorrier state.

Losing Streak

Binding all the various threads of my experience together was a profound sense of loss: loss of open roads, loss of a relationship, loss of vigour, loss of interest, loss of 'success', loss of possibilities, even loss of my denial-fuelled cover story about going travelling. Loss is a crucial contributor to depression. It inhabits our thoughts like darkness fills a room when we turn off the light.

Depression arises when we perceive we have lost something of significance, perhaps something we judge to be essential to our happiness or future well-being. Our mind quietly latches on to a host of connected meanings, such as pessimistic views of the future and negative conceptions of the self ('I'm a loser'). Such is the misdirected power of the brooding mind that it rarely stops at our actual losses. Generating hypothetical losses, reasons for why we will forever remain disappointed, and all-new personal histories that rubbish our every action are just some of its machinations.

The medium in which this largely unconscious process takes place is, of course, thought. Thinking plays a critical (literally!) role in depression. Much of this book is implicitly dedicated to the investigation of the fascinating little entities that we call thoughts.

The Bigger Picture

Not all depressions are reactive – that is, precipitated by events in a person's life. The factors that give rise to an episode of depression, or even a tendency towards it, can be manifold. The onset of depression is often unclear because it can be so gradual.

Genetics, brain function, physical health, age, gender and personality traits can all contribute. But the stuff we are born with need not be an obstacle to living a healthy human life. If you disagree or think differently, pause a moment. Take a look at what might be a spontaneous flurry of negative thinking. Say hello to it and keep on reading.

'Vulnerability to depression' is a common phrase in clinical literature. It implies that some of us are more likely to be depressed than others. I would suggest it is more useful to be interested in your own depression. And to 'own' your enquiries into it. Let go of comparisons and speculations about other people's. Learning about yours is plenty to be getting on with. My Irish hilltop depression was powerful. It changed the whole direction of my life. I can locate it to a time and place, but I cannot pinpoint its beginning and end. I remember the 'symptoms' hung around for months – long after I'd got out of bed, moved house, got a job, had some therapy and apparently fully re-engaged in life. Two decades later, I still experience periods of depression, but they are different now. Back then, I could not see the sky for the clouds. Now I see passing storms more easily and quickly for what they are.

> The abyss of depression is a precious thing. It feels like sadness, like emotional death. But, just as winter isn't the absence of life, but only a stage in the cycle of vitality, feeling low is an essential part of living.
>
> FROM 'SUNBATHING IN THE RAIN'
> Gwyneth Lewis[15]

Processing the Past

Being interested in the narrative of depression is a potentially therapeutic offering to oneself. A mindful approach to working with it does not exclude honouring our life story and all the plotlines and players that comprise it. Counselling and psychotherapy can contribute much here. Making sense of the main causes does not have to mean years of analysis or introspection. Addressing the impact of critical life events is often simpler than we imagine. This frees up emotional space that allows us to move on in life.

For me, psychotherapy was indispensable in helping me make connections between experiences of leaving my home country as a child and resulting confusions about where I belonged. These confusions paradoxically propelled me to travel far and wide. Understanding this was like doing an intricate jigsaw puzzle.

A corner piece was remembering a remark my father had made years earlier – that he thought I was grieving for something when our family moved from Ireland to England.

Gradually, I was able to uncover memories, such as on the day I left my childhood home, when I stood in my near-deserted street, under a grey sky, all of my friends absent, no farewells from anyone – a denial I was departing for ever from the only community I had ever known. I remember noticing how one passing, younger boy seemed to have become 'grown up' in a way that seemed profoundly odd. The 'story of my life' becomes discontinuous at this point, as if part of me is still stuck back on that street. I have since made incalculable use of this one memory. The stuckness remains, but the emotional pain of losing a home has gone.

To shed flecks of light on some contributory factors to your depression is enough.

Once you have some basic connections, the smart bit is to resist wallowing there. Carefully file away your knowledge and get on with the task of living. Giving priority to one's life here and now is a hallmark of the mindful approach. Allow the past to play second fiddle. It is gone for good. Its use can only be in the service of living now.

CHAPTER TWO

Finding a Foothold, Clearing a Path

The first steps out of depression lie in recognizing how it works and acting skilfully to undo its inflexible grasp. We need to find ways to become unstuck, and give ourselves good reasons to try. Our attitude plays a decisive part in this effort. Depression is an opportunity to learn, or relearn, the art of taking care of ourselves. Knowing what matters, honouring our limits and paying attention to how we put in the time are what give life much-needed momentum.

Travels on the Tragic Roundabout

One of the most debilitating things about depression is the confusion it fosters within the mind. Cast adrift from treasured feelings of normality, we lose touch with routines, interests and modes of being that give life a sense of ownership and structure.

Time becomes muddled when we experience future adversities as if they are happening now – such is the power of negative thoughts when we focus on them. Day feels like night, and vice versa, when sleep patterns fall into disorder. Eating becomes erratic – we have a hateful disinterest in food one moment and over-indulge the next. Contact with other human beings is impeded by our inner turmoil. Devoid of spontaneous desire or willpower, we slide into states of inertia, leaving us feeling dazed and disorientated.

Depression is like wearing darkly tinted glasses. Everything appears blacker than it is. You cannot perceive the subtleties of form and movement. Unable to see clearly, you become disinterested. The world in turn appears more distant and disagreeable. Your projections become your truth.

Night of the Living Dead

One night, trapped in the ghostly realm of the insomniac, I stood by my window, watching people talking at a bus stop across the road from my house. I'd been in a black hole for days and felt crushed by the previous three hours lying in the dark, waiting for sleep that wouldn't come. Now I became a peripheral observer of the lives of others.

They might as well have been a different species. I was dumbfounded by their abilities to sit, stand, walk and talk. I huddled against the window frame in awe at their spontaneous interactions. It was as if they were alive in ways I had never known. From my solitary world behind glass, relating to my environment felt as possible as taking a trip to Neptune.

Seeing How it Works

To step out of depression is to disengage from the inner spin of self-perpetuating mental, emotional and behavioural processes that conspire to leave us feeling disconnected from ourselves and others. As with most of life's problems, the solution lies in understanding the basic mechanism of the problem.

When we get depressed, we feel sad. We may also be troubled by feelings of anxiety and irritability about our sadness, or guilt about letting others down. We may even lose our ability to react emotionally at all. Our emotional reactions, combined with our inability to reverse the impact of whatever triggered the depression, lead us to focus more on our sense of loss or failure to match up to our own standards. This reinforces the feelings of sadness.

Vicious Circles

Interest in life wanes as it becomes increasingly difficult to enjoy normal activities. Cut off from ordinary pleasures, we withdraw from them. This is understandable but offers less chance of reward or positive feedback. Withdrawing and avoiding merely increase our preoccupation with how bad we feel and how unsolvable our problems appear. Negative thoughts become more frequent and intense. We are less inclined to take events at face value and more inclined to misinterpret them in ways that are biased against ourselves.

Physical functioning (sleep, appetite, sex drive) may also be disturbed, further contributing to our feel-bad state. In vain efforts to fend off feeling depressed, we may turn to alcohol, drugs or food. Such action delivers, at best, a temporary escape into numbness before a further emotional downturn.

Seen in this way, depression is a series of chain reactions. Each element feeds back to the others, strengthening the low mood and creating a vicious cycle. The more depressed we become, the more depressing thoughts we think, and the more we believe them. The worse we feel, the less we do, and the worse we feel. Expecting negative outcomes offers no motivation to act and every reason to avoid acting, so goals become unrealized and life meaningless. We turn away from painful emotions only to end up feeling less alive. With every spin of this carousel, we meet the unpleasant consequences of our own psychology. Might we try a different ride?

Becoming Unstuck

Languishing in undemanding places is a depressive's favourite pastime. Consider the bed – commonly a symbol of retreat from active engagement with life. How little the duvet asks of me, how much it promises, if I just carry on lying here...

I tell myself there's really no point in getting up... that I won't enjoy anything... that it'll only make me feel worse... that life sucks and then you die. Stop! Look! Can I see this merry-go-round for what it is: the churning of the dejected mind, the allure of withdrawal and avoidance? Can I let go of their meagre comforts and short-lived pay-offs?

Experience tells me I will soon be bulldozed by lethargy and rumination. To step out of this mental quagmire requires the simplest of postural shifts, just enough to untangle an indolent mind from a dead weight of a body.

Galvanized into action by one effortless act of will, I discover myself rising, casting off this shroud of a duvet, pulling back the curtains and becoming enveloped in light. The upsurge of physical energy is already palpable. These simple bodily movements have terrific momentum. They take me towards life, rather than away from it. The bed has already lost its charm. The world becomes a place of possibilities again.

The Imperative of Mindfulness

Notice that this simple movement, from a place of stuckness to one of relative freedom, originates in the mind. The movement

> Insanity: doing the same thing over and over again and expecting different results.
>
> ALBERT EINSTEIN (1879–1955)
> Physicist

is made possible by paying attention. First, there is the registering of what is occurring ('Stop! Look!') and the recollecting of potential hazards ('lethargy and rumination'). Then, the actualizing of an intention ('effortless act of will') that sidesteps these hazards. This, in a nutshell, is the transformative effect of the mental quality, or attitude, we call mindfulness.

The word 'mindfulness' is not easy to define, but it conveys something of our innate ability to be fully attentive to what is happening in the present moment, rather than operating on 'automatic', in such a way that we create space for change to occur. The rest of this chapter is dedicated to taking care of our moment-to-moment experience by cultivating a sharper awareness of it, and imbuing it with well-intentioned action.

How to Make a Step Change

If our internal pain is determining our outward actions, the chances are we are not taking good care of ourselves. Depression encourages us to hang out in places of limited potential, such as beds and sofas, but these are the very places that can rob us of the mood-lifting fruits of activity.

Understanding that 'depressed behaviour' is often a futile and counter-productive attempt to escape unwanted thoughts and feelings suggests we need to act differently. We would also do well to focus less on the gloomy projections of the mind and more on listening to the wisdom of our experience. Even in the deepest emotional troughs, when our wisdom affirms that curling up in a corner is the best or only option, we need to grasp the indispensability of mobilizing and acting as soon as our energy returns. Otherwise we run the risk, as the poet Gwyneth Lewis put it, of getting eaten alive by time.

Breaking the Pattern

To break the hard edges of a depressive vicious circle and reinstate an active life requires consideration, effort and the willingness to follow through on wise intentions. This is easier to do than your thinking mind will have you believe! To aid this process, try posing yourself these questions:

- What activities in my life have given me a sense of purpose?
- How would I be spending my time if I wasn't depressed?
- What activities do I know make me feel better about myself, which are not rooted in attempts to stay out of contact with unpleasant thoughts, emotions and body sensations?
- How can I reinstate activities, step by step, which have the potential to give me enjoyment or a sense of accomplishment, regardless of what my negative thoughts might be saying now?

- If I am struggling with outer demands, as well as inner ones, how can I create a healthy balance of personal space and more fulfilling interactions with my environment?

Spend time considering these questions and revisit them as often as you can. They all distil into one exercise: compiling a list of mood-lifting activities. Try to come up with activities that fall into different domains: physical (bodily movement and exercise), creative (employing the imagination), social (contact with other humans), and nature (contact with animals and outdoor environments).

A World of Possibilities

Create as large a list as possible and include everything you can think of, no matter how small. Don't store this list in your head – write it down! Keeping a written record helps to solidify half-formed ideas and provides much-needed 'head space'. Add to your list every time a new idea comes to mind so that your list becomes a living, evolving compendium of possibilities.

Each day, decide which activities you can incorporate into your daily routine. Start gradually by choosing one or two activities and allotting them a time. Then, regardless of how you feel, just do them. If you notice any resistance or self-criticism, consider these a sign that you are working gently against depressive tendencies and keep going. Don't be afraid to experiment with the length and frequency of activities but do stick to your daily plan. Review how you feel afterwards.

Taking Care of the Small Stuff

Seasoning the minutes and hours with regular activity is a direct step out of the morass of depression, where waiting to feel like wanting to do something is like waiting for your wildest dreams to come true. Trust in the mood-lifting power of well-intentioned action comes with acting, not with sitting around thinking about acting!

It is vital to treat yourself with care and kindness in this process. Unbinding from depressed states is about considering the means over the ends. It is about taking care of the seconds and minutes and being less concerned with future outcomes. It is about keeping in mind that small actions matter. It is about trying out new things, or doing old things differently, for no other reason than to see what happens. It's about knowing when to stop and rest. It is about remembering to commend yourself for giving something a go.

Pulling the Plug

Someone I know who was suffering from depression recalled his behaviour at the time as 'switching off'. He described his creeping realization that he had 'pulled the plug' on previously cherished aspects of his life. He had stopped listening to music when driving, despite always enjoying this. Next, he gave up using his music equipment at home. Then, his car lay stationary because he stopped driving. This 'switching off' progressed to an ever-widening range of activities and culminated in him terminating all social contact.

> **GREEN SPACE**
>
> According to a major research study, just five minutes of daily outdoor activity in any green space can significantly boost a person's mood, self-esteem and mental health. The researchers found that exercising in wilderness areas or near water tended to have the biggest impact on mental state.[16]

Noticing the impact of his actions was the turning point. In seeing how his mood and his behaviour interacted and influenced each other, he was able to figure out healthier ways of conducting his time. He prescribed for himself a course of pressing 'on' buttons on a regular basis. Repeating small, simple actions – flicking switches – was the primary means to bringing him back to life.

Switching the Lights Back On

In the months following my Irish hilltop depression, switching the inner lights back on took various forms. There was the 'macro' stuff, like getting a job and moving house, which provided energy and structure. But it was the subtler changes that proved to be the most nourishing. I noticed how cycling into the countryside revitalized me, physically and emotionally.

On long rides, I discovered the importance of attending to the journey rather than the destination. I would refuse to be captivated by the horizon and overwhelmed by thoughts about how far I had to go. I learned to refocus on the forward motion of the bike, the rotation of the pedals, the shifting ground beneath me, the inclination in a chosen direction. I learned to imbue other spheres of life with this attitude.

I sought out people who exhibited a sensitivity towards the 'inner life' and who were less beguiled by popular ideas of happiness as something that is found outside of oneself. I rediscovered the importance of connecting with other human beings – sharing experiences and talking honestly and openly about what mattered to me. I learned to let go of the past by honouring painful memories rather than trying to shut them out through idle distraction and sensual indulgence.

I began to relish the work of poets who seemed able to wrench meaning from existence. Art became a catalyst for challenging unwitting notions that existence was some static, homogenous burden I had been unfairly lumbered with.

A Positive Spin

In each moment of our lives, what we are in contact with affects us. Contact can be with anything happening through our five senses, in our bodies, with emotions, and with our thinking processes: the myriad interpretations, imaginings and fantasies of the mind.

> **CONNECTING WITH LIFE**
>
> Take a moment to notice the things that you are in contact with now – thoughts, feelings, sights, sounds, smells, physical sensations, urges, memories, fantasies, plans, imaginings.

Contact is a dynamic process and one that is rapidly shifting and modifying from moment to moment. It is a given in life. As we are psycho-physical organisms interacting with our environment, we cannot fail to be in contact.

In depression, the inclination is to be in contact with painful feelings, states of physical inertia and negative thoughts. These are all self-perpetuating and mutually reinforcing. Like the trace effects of a bad dream after waking, they lend a melancholic atmosphere to our lived experience.

Understanding depression as an active process allows us to disengage from it by changing what we make contact with. Hence the value of weaving in purposeful activity. By changing what we do, we foster a more wholesome and invigorating relationship with our external world. In turn, we inherit the fruits of our actions.

Coming Up With the Goods

It is essential to consolidate the effects of positive action. Keeping a detailed daily record of the good things that happen is a surprisingly powerful way of doing this. This encourages you to notice and retain the numerous agreeable and satisfying

> In the depths of winter, I finally learned
> that within me there lay an invincible summer.
>
> FROM 'RETURN TO TIPASA'
> Albert Camus (1913–1960)[17]

events that might normally pass you by. Let your record be one to cherish. Dedicate a special notebook to it. Allow this to be a living receptacle of all good things.

Recollecting and recording the positives of life is about noticing the small stuff: the smile of a passer-by, the sound of a bird, a pleasant smell, a chore completed, a stimulating conversation, a happy memory, a smooth journey, an obstacle overcome. Any moment of achievement, enjoyment or lightness of being, no matter how minor or fleeting, should go into your notebook. It doesn't matter what you notice; the important thing is to hold it in mind. Otherwise you will likely discount, dismiss or overlook the experience.

The Brain Game

It is true that our negative evaluations of self, situation and future are deeply embedded through depressive mental habits. But focusing on the positive helps to counterbalance an even deeper negativity bias – that of the human brain itself.

Humans are like any other animals in seeking safety and protection in an uncertain and often dangerous world. One way in which our minds have learned to deal with this is by giving preferential treatment to negative occurrences over positive ones.

Neuropsychologist and meditation teacher Rick Hanson compares the way the brain scans, registers, stores and recalls the events of our lives to being 'like Velcro for negative experiences and Teflon for positive ones.'[18] The success of our genes has depended on our ancestors overestimating threats to their well-being and underestimating their abilities to cope with adversity. Despite the fact that most of us live at the top of the food chain these days, our brains still work as if having our daily bread might require a fight to the death.

Enjoying the Moment

Painful stuff grabs our attention more readily than pleasant, which often glides by unacknowledged. To recalibrate this negativity bias, explains Hanson, we must focus on the positive and savour it: 'Make it last by staying with it for 5, 10, even 20 seconds; don't let your attention skitter off to something else.'[19]

Taking in the positives is all part of the quiet revolution of mindfulness – bringing awareness to the flow of life, seeing more clearly what is happening, and holding on to the nuggets that come our way. Note that this practice is not about disregarding the pain and uncertainties of life. It's about developing a more balanced sense of pleasant and unpleasant. Each of us is hard-wired to be on the lookout for the painful

> Focus on your emotions and body sensations, since these are the essence of implicit memory. Let the experience fill your body and be as intense as possible. For example, if someone is good to you, let the feeling of being cared about bring warmth to your whole chest.
>
> FROM 'BUDDHA'S BRAIN'
> Rick Hanson & Richard Mendius[20]

and difficult. It's the positive stuff that, depressed or not, we've been screening out and it needs some generous attention.

Great Divides

Stepping out of depression is not just about taking action. It is also about cultivating a habit of healthy stopping. The interludes between activities are the punctuation points of our lives. These offer opportunities for reflection and digestion of experience.

Bringing awareness to the transition times between activities helps us pace our movements throughout the day. We are better able to ground ourselves after periods of busyness. If life is a journey then these interludes are the park benches where we can sit, rest, and decide our next move.

A JOURNEY IN SPACE

- Sitting or standing, allow your body to become still. Give yourself full permission to achieve nothing for the next couple of minutes. Bring your awareness to this process of stopping. Take a few deep breaths, then allow your breath to be free. Relax.
- Notice the space in your surroundings. Usually we notice the things that take up space. In a room, we tend to see only the contents: objects, people, walls. To notice space means to become aware of the gaps between objects. Allow your attention to find these gaps – the emptiness of your surroundings.
- Space is always present, yet it rarely attracts the attention. It exists around, and within, your body. If you are in a room right now, consider how it too exists in a wider space. Space is not just part of your environment. Space is what contains your environment.
- Space has a calming quality. It is peaceful in a way that objects – animate or inanimate – often are not, since these tend to arouse reactions within us. Space offers no resistance. By its nature, it doesn't get in your way. When you move, it moves with you. It is always there.

Inspired by the teachings of the Buddhist monk Ajahn Sumedho

Minding the Gaps

When depressed, reinstating meaningful and mood-enhancing activities needs to be counterbalanced with intervals of rest. If we are not careful, focusing our efforts on 'doing' alone can depreciate into unconscious attempts to avoid painful feelings. Even worse, holding unrealistic expectations of what we are capable of can translate into relentless striving and self-berating. So creating pockets of space in the day, when we cut loose from inner and outer demands, has to be a priority. We can do this by intentionally pausing between tasks to absorb the impact of our actions and discern how they have contributed to our overall mood.

Valuing Life

Attitude towards self, others, world and future plays a major part in our life, whether we are depressed or not. Our behaviour and physicality reveal much about our attitude at any one time. Are we passively dwelling in customary states of blunt attention and dull awareness, or genuinely alive to our experience in the moment?

One evening, I was sitting on the top deck of a bus that was zooming through some rain-soaked streets. I dwelled in a comfortable dullness. Unable to see out of the steamed-up windows, my attention hovered complacently amidst a haze of flitting thoughts and images – that semi-trance state of a passenger content to be carried from one place to another. My whole body lolled as it was swept along by the swaying motion of the bus.

I was stirred from this reverie by the sight of a young woman ascending the stairs, scanning the deck for a seat and aiming herself for one at the front of the bus. Each one of her movements was purposeful: how she eagerly claimed her seat, flung off her coat with near-passionate conviction, and leaned forwards to enthusiastically rub the condensation from the bus's front window with her sleeve, as if she were about to arm-wrestle her reflection. Even from eight rows back, her spirit was unmistakable. It was as if she wasn't just riding on that bus, but propelling it forwards. Noticing how she was conducting her journey helped me to waken up to my own.

The Bottom Line

How we approach life has as much potential to shape and maintain a depression as to undermine one. For depression has the power to rob us of meaning and overwhelm us with the urge to withdraw. In so doing, we can get hijacked by lethargy, fear and doubt, and led away from what we most value. How to strike a balance between honouring feelings of loss and hopelessness that play their part in the deeper alchemy of the healing process while, at the same time, staying connected to what truly matters to us?

The answer lies in exploring our personal values. It is these that form the core of what is important to us as human beings: our heart's deepest desires; the meaning(s) of life itself.

> Happiness is not a state to arrive at,
> but a manner of travelling.
> MARGARET LEE RUNBECK (1905–1956)
> Writer[21]

Values are the guiding principles that quietly pull us like a magnet towards our future. Sometimes that magnetic pull is strong, sometimes not. We never achieve our values. Rather they are the qualities that can underpin our actions in this world. Values are, by their nature, personal and, therefore, chosen. In language form, they can be any word or phrase that represents something subjectively vital and beautiful.

Freshly Mined Gold

No one can tell you what your values are. Deep down, you already know. If you have not consciously considered them before, now is the time. Trust that even in the mini-death of depression, when nothing feels like it could ever matter, your values quietly abide, waiting to be picked up like freshly mined gold on a dark night. This is one of the concealed gifts of depression: through plunging to the depths of isolation and despair, you are obliged to reconsider the nature and direction of your life and connect with what holds true worth for you.

Taking a Compass Bearing

I recall a moment standing by a road, drinking orange juice, on a hilltop overlooking my adopted home town. It was a cold, clear autumn day nearing twilight. I had been cycling and was taking a break before the final miles home.

Only fragments remain in memory now: the taste of the juice on my teeth; how the bike leaned against a fence at an angle; how the low, November light danced softly around my eyelashes and seemed to warm my thoughts.

The thoughts were about the future. Not about the trip home, or the day or week ahead. This was thinking with a long lens: where did this life I was living go next? It was pushing a year since my meltdown in the Irish hills. My mood was brighter. The destructive force of those black holes had made way for comparatively benign grey skies and occasional rainstorms. Sunny spells were not uncommon.

My life was different now and, outwardly at least, progressing. But progressing how, and to where? Question marks formed in my mind like the brightest stars gently emerging in the sky above me.

I had no answers, but I remember the wild and limitless span of my imagination, and a compelling sense that life was about unknowable horizons, change and growth. Stirring within me was an examination of the priorities of life and the extent of my willingness to embrace them. It felt as though my heart was urging my head to realize its potential, except my head wasn't fluent in the language of the heart.

The Necessity of Inner Work

Undercutting this confusion was the imperative of learning the lessons of depression: that psychological well-being trumps every other concern in life bar physical survival; that developing a healthy relationship to life is, ultimately, about being on good terms with oneself. I sensed a clear and vital need to prosper inwardly at all costs.

As I finished the day's journey, living well seemed all that mattered. This insight was a hint that I was migrating out of the wastelands of depression. I was grateful for that, but instinctively knew there was much work to do. Inner work.

I recollected a friend's comment about the priceless nature of acceptance and understanding. I intuited how no amount of material comfort, security or success could deliver lasting peace of mind. I toyed with next moves and new possibilities, inward journeys, outward journeys. What to do? Where, and how? Big questions. Like I say, I had no answers.

What Do You Stand For?

To explore one's values is the act of a sophisticated, self-aware being who is not solely driven by the blind forces of biological survival and procreation. To explore one's values is to sensitively locate where you find meaning in life.

> **LIFE MATTERS**
>
> Numerous scientific studies conclude that lottery winners don't end up much happier than the rest of us. Life satisfaction is determined less by material acquisition and more by a sense of meaning, purpose, personal growth, healthy relationships and self-acceptance.

This can be done in any way you choose, such as through contemplation, dialogue, self-enquiry or artistic expression. The method is not the point. The point is to give time to explore what really matters to you.

To get underway, try asking yourself these questions:

- If I had a month to live, how would I spend that time? What is it about those things I would choose that have meaning and worth for me?
- What or who do I draw inspiration from in life now? What are the qualities and attributes I discern in those things or in those people?
- Who do I dislike in life? What lies beneath this dislike? If I were that person, what is it I would do differently? How would I manifest that change? What would be different as a result? What does this tell me about my values?
- If I won a large fortune tomorrow, what would I do with my wealth? Who would I involve in my life? What do these choices tell me about what's important to me?

- If I achieved my goals in life, what would this change about my life? How would I act from then on? How would I relate to people? What would be different about how I conducted my life? What qualities underlie these actions?

A Shared Wish

What results from your enquiry can only be a symbolic expression of your personal values – words, images, ideas, perhaps a 'felt-sense' – and not the values themselves. Remember that values can never be captured, only lived by and for. They are like distant stars or compass points that orientate you on your life's journey.

Ultimately, all values share common roots of connection and compassion. They epitomize humanity's shared wish to live with contentment, health and happiness. In this way, values merge effortlessly with mindfulness practice, which is about attuning to our immediate experience and relating to the world with clarity and open-heartedness.

Establishing a Path

If our values give us our bearings and our actions propel us forwards, then mindfulness is the manner in which we may travel. The path of mindfulness is less concerned with goals and destinations and more with the style and tone of the journey.

FROM HERE TO WHERE?

• Choose a quiet place where you won't be disturbed. Sitting or standing, allow your body to relax and settle.

• Notice how your body has a direction. It always faces one way. So, too, with your life, which moves in one direction.

• To get to this point in your life, here and now, you had to make choices. Many choices. Review some you have made recently. Do you see any pattern in the steps you have taken?

• We each have our characteristic ways of moving through life. Taking a step towards something means taking a step away from something else. We can never get everything we want. Meanwhile, the world changes with every choice we make and with every step we take.

• What steps in life have you taken so far for which you can offer yourself warm appreciation? Are there choices you regret having made? Are there any you regret not having made?

• We each have our own different ways of avoiding things. Can you be aware of what you have been avoiding so far?

• Notice how you feel. Take note of what is occurring in your body, and with emotions and thoughts. Notice your relationship to the world around you. Notice your relationship to your sense of self.

• Before making your next move, try to get in touch with the process that is going on inside you. Are you doing what you really want to do? Where are you taking your life next?

Paying attention to experience in the here and now is the priority. Bringing awareness to what is unfolding in body, heart, mind and world, moment to moment, fosters an intimacy with life that is impossible when we are in thrall to the multiple plans perpetuated by our restless minds.

In the sense that mindfulness is about creating space, the metaphor of a path is a rich one. For what is a path but a space – a channel that allows free movement and safe passage, unencumbered by obstacles. A path, therefore, is an absence as much as a presence, suggesting something of the mysterious, immaterial terrain to which mindfulness takes us. Writer Stephen Batchelor, who has explored the nuances of the metaphor of a path with great lucidity, articulates its emptiness as 'that open and unfettered space that frees us to respond from a liberating perspective rather than react from a fixed position.'[22]

At the same time, a path is also something that has been cultivated – brought into being – by others who have trodden the same track before you. In turn, you maintain it for those coming behind you. In this sense, a path is, as Batchelor puts it, 'carved from commitment and opened up by letting go. It entails both doing something and allowing something to happen. A path is both a task and a gift.'[23]

Breaking the Vicious Cycle

In terms of depression, if there is one thing to hold in mind about the significance of the metaphor of a path, it's this: one step matters. To illustrate this, consider depression to be rather like a baggage carousel (the things you find in the arrivals hall of an airport) that is teeming with every negative thought, unpleasant feeling, and avoidant, counterproductive action you've ever experienced. The whole lot is piled high and heavy, sagging and leaning into each other. The carousel chugs away, hauling this load around on a continuous loop.

When you find yourself deposited amidst all that baggage, no matter which direction you move on that carousel you will keep encountering the same old contents. You don't get anywhere new. What can you do? The answer is obvious: step off the carousel. Simple and effective. Now you're standing on steady ground and no longer entangled in all that oppressive content. With one precious step you have given yourself the freedom to move in a new direction. You have created a path.

A Different Journey

A path of mindfulness is, by nature, an inner path: a voyage of discovery conducted by and for the heart and mind. This path is brought into being through a search for contentment, a need to resolve suffering, or both.

Whatever the motivation, this movement inwards – an exploration of subjective experience – can have profound effects on our outer actions and our relationship to the world. The next chapter addresses these matters, which comprise the essence of mindfulness practice.

> Whether in search of food, work, safety, or meaning, we set out on trails left by others or blaze trails of our own. Whenever we leave our mark – be it on a physical or cultural landscape – we allow the possibility of a path to emerge.
>
> FROM 'LIVING WITH THE DEVIL'
> Stephen Batchelor[24]

As for me, in the days following my roadside self-enquiry, in some ways I did nothing new. I took a trip. As a seasoned traveller, well practised in the art of reducing the material contents of life to a small rucksack and a finite wad of traveller's cheques, it was no radical step to book a one-way flight from London to Istanbul. It was a bigger deal to set myself the additional task of an onward, land-based journey in midwinter to the poorest state in India. This was as much a pragmatic decision as it was an indication I was ready to create a valued direction for myself. Even so, the potential pitfalls of repeating fruitless patterns of 'running away' and novelty-seeking – not to mention the disconnection from job, career, family, friends – hung painfully in mind. Fear arose at thoughts of how this plan might blow up in my face.

New Leads

Perhaps what propelled me forth was my own version of a question I later found out is regularly encountered by mindfulness practitioners: Is it possible to do the same old stuff in life but have a different relationship to it?

> Suffering ceases to be suffering
> at the moment it finds a meaning.
>
> FROM 'MAN'S SEARCH FOR MEANING'
> Viktor E. Frankl[25]

What made my trip different to previous ones were its purpose and its function. It was inspired, paradoxically, by the need to journey inside, steered by values of self-acceptance and understanding. It had been triggered by a friend passing me a leaflet about a mindfulness meditation retreat, run in eastern India by Western teachers. It was further helped along by my lack of knowledge of anything similar closer to home. Unlike previous trips, this one was less charged with excitement and achievement and instead more concerned with knowledge and compassion.

Journeying four and a half thousand miles by land in one month was a final fling for my restless travelling tendencies, I told myself, before I would dedicate myself to a different kind of pursuit. As with a lot of things in life, it only made partial sense at the time. In retrospect, it seems like a long way to go to sit on a cushion and close my eyes…

> Do not ignore the effect of right action, saying, 'This will come to nothing'. A pitcher is filled with water by a steady stream of drops; likewise, the wise person improves and achieves well-being a little at a time.
>
> THE BUDDHA[26]

CHAPTER THREE

Fresh Prints on an Old Trail

We have all the time in the world to notice one breath. How easy it is not to! But if we overlook such simple and immediate realities, we lose touch with the vital, fluid nature of life. A direct way of reconnecting with the great occurrence that is the present moment is the cultivation of mindfulness. This ordinary mental quality is the dynamic factor of a long-established path that leads to well-being. Finding this path and walking it are not separate.

Hallo There

Right here, right now, is life. The present moment is your one chance to be fully alive to your experience, the only point from which you can foster awareness of what is happening as it is happening. Everything else is history or fantasy – some form of mental construction of past or future.

Despite the ever-available present, it's easy to overlook. Take right now. What exactly is going on? As you read these words, your experience is a visual consciousness of black squiggles on a cream background and the spontaneous meaning-making produced by your mind as it interprets them. Light is reflecting off these squiggles, invisibly impressing their image on the retinas of your eyes, generating signals to your brain, and precipitating reactions, such as thoughts and feelings. Your experience is, therefore, constantly changing – it is different, in some immeasurable way, to how it was when you started reading this paragraph.

Conditional Statements

How is this experience coming about? The fact that you are reading these words (and that I wrote them) is easily taken for granted. Yet both are conditioned by a multitude of factors. Firstly, there's your entire life story, and everything that led up to you being right here, right now, with this book. The same goes for me, up to the point I wrote this sentence. Could we ever have planned or predicted this momentary encounter between 'you' and 'me'?

And what about our medium of communication: this book? It's another miracle of circumstances, brought into being by countless human activities, raw materials and manufacturing processes. It was once, in part, a tree, which needed light, rain and soil, themselves conditioned by other elements. The same law of conditionality that brought this book into existence operates for everything and everyone around you. And everything occurring within you, too.

This remarkable process is happening all the time. It's a process we can be awake to. A mindful approach to life does not require an *analysis* of the ever-changing conditions of our existence, but it does invite a penetrating inquiry into its raw immediacy. The only time and the only place from which this inquiry can be made are 'here' and 'now', respectively. At this elusive intersection of timeless space lies the path of mindfulness and the freshness and vitality it offers into our lives.

JUST STANDING

- Pick a quiet place where you won't be disturbed. For the next five minutes give yourself completely to not having to go anywhere or do anything.
- Stand naturally, with your feet hip-width apart, toes pointing forwards and arms by your sides. Allow your back to be upright while respecting the natural curvature of your spine. Head poised on top, allow your eyes to gaze softly at a point on the floor about ten feet in front of you. Take two or three deep in-breaths, letting the breath flow out in its own time, then allow the breath to return to its natural rhythm.
- Gently compose your mind on the vertical sense of the body. Its uprightness. The natural ease of simply standing.
- Notice the sensations of contact between the feet and the floor. The ground supports you, holds you upright. You don't need to do anything to be connected to the earth.
- Become aware of the body as a whole. Tune into the total experience of the body, with its many, varied sensations and feelings. Notice, too, what thoughts and moods are present. Cultivate an overall sense of what is happening 'inside'.
- Become aware of everything around and beyond the body. Tune into the senses of seeing, hearing, touching and smelling. Cultivate an overall sense of what is happening 'outside'.
- Now become aware of 'inside' and 'outside' together.
- Notice how what is 'inside' and what is 'outside' effortlessly merge together. Allow this sense of balance between 'inner' and 'outer' to be as it is. There is no need to acquire, fix or maintain it.

Defining the Undefinable

Much has been written, spoken and pondered regarding this thing called mindfulness. As a quality of mind and a 'way of being', mindfulness cannot adequately be confined to, or defined by, a set of words. You will never acquire a fully satisfactory understanding of it from any book, including this one.

In squiggle form, the best I can do is this: Mindfulness is an alert yet receptive awareness. It is a particular way of paying attention to what is happening in the mind and body, as it is occurring. It exerts a stabilizing and regulating effect on the mind by countering sensory distraction. It brings a quality of breadth to experience – an awareness of things in relation to things. Mindfulness is, therefore, both a 'presence of mind' that monitors experience, and a connective awareness of what is happening to us, and in us, from moment to moment. Such a way of being is sustained by qualities of interest, warmth and patience. As an attitude, it is about approaching life in a kindly, spacious and non-discriminating way.

Mindfulness is an inherent and versatile quality of human consciousness. You don't need to acquire it because you've already got it. The *practice* of mindfulness is, therefore, merely the development of your innate capacity to be aware. Rather than trying to get somewhere, or achieve something, mindfulness is more about 'coming home'.

Lucid Moments

To get a better sense of what a mindful experience is, consider its opposite: a mindless one. Mindlessness is that common state of being mentally scattered, preoccupied with past and future and generally getting 'stuck in your head'. Such a state is, by its nature, not something you are aware of at the time. It's like walking into a room to get something, only to realize you've forgotten what it is you went there to get. You made the journey as if on autopilot – you can recall little about it and even less about why you set out in the first place.

Mindfulness, on the other hand, brings a brightness and stability to experience. Its hallmarks are calmness, clarity and non-reactivity: a mind that can 'stand back' to observe momentary phenomena rather than interfere with them. It is a lucid awareness of what is happening at all levels of body, heart and mind. Being mindful, then, is that ability to be both a fully engaged participant *and* a clearly discerning observer in one's life. It's about walking into a room with a clarity of purpose, aware of the soft fall of each foot on the carpet, the feel of the air, the mood of one's mind… It's about being awake to what's going on.

To adopt this participant-observer 'position' suggests something of a paradox because it implies an open-hearted connection to subjective experience that is mixed with a kind of semi-detachment to it. Mindfulness is full of such paradoxes, which words will never crack.

Va-va-voom

The word 'mindfulness' is somewhat of a misnomer because it has nothing to do with mind-fullness. As an attitude and a practice, it is about sparseness and simplicity rather than saturation or embellishment. With mindfulness, less is always more. This essence is captured by the tiny, 2,500-year-old, Indian word *va*, meaning 'just', 'only' or 'simply'. *Va* is the word used by the historical Buddha, a man called Siddhattha Gotama (fifth century BCE), to express the quality of bare and unelaborated 'seeing' that is characteristic of, and necessary for, mindfulness practice.

Va is the attribute of bringing 'nothing extra' to the task in hand. For to *just* pay attention is to be in *direct* contact with what is being observed, untainted by mental labelling, judging and subjective bias. *Va* implies a more objective stance towards one's experience. Without all our habitual mental reactions and projections, we can see things as they truly are.

This is the kind of seeing that, in the visual sense, we all do as small children, when we come across an interesting object for the first time. With a mix of infant curiosity and astonishment, we become absorbed in studying it. We have no name for this 'thing', and no past or current associations with it. There are no complications to cloud our perception. We see the object in the freshest way possible. To be mindful is, therefore, to have a child's-eye view of the world – to see things as if for the first time.

THE CLANGERS

One of my favourite instructions for cultivating mindfulness is from an episode of the children's BBC TV series, *The Clangers*. This is about a family of small, wool-knitted creatures living on a hollow, blue planet in faraway space. The narrator seeks to arouse the viewer's curiosity in the adventures of these bizarre little fellows with this kindly invitation: 'Let us go very close. Let us look and listen very carefully. And perhaps we will see. And hear.'

How's It Going So Far?

While reading this book, have there been occasions when you've suddenly noticed that, although you thought you were reading the words and taking them in, your attention had actually wandered to something else entirely? And then you realized that you couldn't remember the last bit you read?

Perhaps you decided to retrace your steps. Maybe you went back a few words, or lines (or even paragraphs) and read them again? And then you discovered that they were vaguely familiar? If this happened to you, please note that it's a very common experience and there's nothing wrong with you. In fact, well spotted for noticing that your mind had wandered!

Here's what happened. You definitely experienced those words/lines/paragraphs, otherwise how could they be familiar? But you weren't aware of them. Experience and awareness are different. The word 'experience' comes from the Latin *experiri*, meaning 'to try'. The word 'awareness' comes from the Greek *horan*, which means 'to see'. Experience implies participating in an event while awareness implies an observation, or overview, of that participation.

So, on one level, you engaged with those 'missing' words but, on another level, you didn't. During those moments, the aware part of you failed to show up. This is mindlessness in action. By contrast, that moment you 'woke up' to the fact that you had drifted, you assumed a position of both participant *and* observer. This is mindfulness in action.

Past Connections

You might presume that mindfulness is solely concerned with the present moment. Yet it is also deeply connected to memory. When we are mindful, we are able to hold things in mind. It is only the remembering of what we are attending to that enables us to maintain an unwavering attention to it.

Consider again the example of drifting off while reading this book. When you realized your mind had wandered and you reconnected with what was actually going on, you had again remembered what it was you were supposed to be doing. In one magical moment, you stitched together your past, present and future into one secure and cohesive unity: directly seeing

TEA MEDITATION

- Take a cup. What is its shape and colour? What is its texture? Choose your tea. Where does it come from? What is in it?
- Now listen to the sound of the water boiling. Give it your full attention. Listen to how the sound changes once the water has boiled.
- Watch the water as you pour it into the cup. Try not to spill even one drop. If you add other things to the tea, notice the patterns and colours that are generated by your actions.
- Breathe in the scent of the tea. Are there different scents – stronger ones, weaker ones? What emotional reactions do you experience?
- Pick up the cup slowly. Notice its weight. Feel its temperature. Feel the steam on your face.
- Take a small sip of tea. Notice what is happening inside your mouth – the movement of your tongue and jaw, the texture and temperature of the liquid, your perception of the tea's flavour.
- Swallow. How does that feel? What is happening in your mouth, throat, chest and belly? Notice the after-taste. Pay attention to how your mind is behaving. Are particular feelings present? Whatever your reactions, simply notice them.
- Wait a moment before taking another sip. Stay slow. See if you can catch the intention to raise the cup to your mouth.
- Continue taking slow sips. Be fully in the moment. Give this tea every ounce of your attention. Notice when the mind drifts into past and future. Gently guide it back each time.

> Something is true only as long as the last person who remembers it.
>
> NAVAJO INDIAN PROVERB

what had happened (past), bringing attention to immediate reality (present), and prospectively reminding yourself to focus again on reading (future).

Modern psychological research has shown that attention comes in discrete moments. That is, we are only able to be attentive to something for the briefest time, after which we have to remind ourselves to keep on being attentive. Mindfulness allows us to bypass the fogginess and forgetfulness our minds are prone to by weaving our attention into a seamless continuity over longer stretches of time. Stabilizing the attention in this way has profoundly calming and clarifying effects. It also allows us to be more awake and 'on guard' to potentially negative and injurious psychological states, such as the ones that depression precipitates. This is why mindfulness has traditionally been understood as a protective mental quality.

A Funny Thing Happened on the Way to the Retreat

It happened years ago, but the memory is still vivid. I was sitting on a stationary bus at the depot. From the window I remember randomly noticing, through a gap between some buildings, that the sky and the sea were the same shade of grey. Then I took a closer look at myself.

It was the start of my epic land voyage east. So far, I'd made the short walk from my house to the bus station to pick up the ride to the airport. I was expectant, thriving in my window seat, waves of excitement and anxiety lapping through my body. In that interval before the bus got moving, two things startled me into a greater self-awareness.

The first was my appearance, reflected in the window. I looked a lot more like a soldier than a tourist. Until now, I hadn't noticed that I was clad head to foot in green. A few days earlier, having heard that temperatures en route to India could plummet to minus 20 degrees in winter, I had panic-bought a hat, coat and thermals from an army surplus shop. I was now wearing the lot along with, for the first time, my green walking boots, my hardy us Marine-edition trousers and a khaki canvas rucksack. This was not a good look for civilian travel at the best of times, and particularly so for crossing politically sensitive borders in the Middle East. But it was a useful lesson in how easy it is to miss what's right under one's nose.

Travels in Inner Space

The second thing that startled me had more momentous consequences. Having grown restless waiting for the bus to depart and bored with the lack of visible demarcation between land and sea, I fished out a book from my daypack (also green). It was an introductory guide to meditation, which I had bought a week earlier, thinking it useful preparation for the retreat. I opened it to page one.

'There are many ways to travel,' began the writer, before cataloguing an extensive variety of modes, methods and speeds of movement. In the second paragraph, he explained, plainly and simply, how physical travel was merely one layer of any human journey; how the mind is never in one place for long; how much of life's grand adventure we miss if we only attend to the external world. He rounded off the paragraph with a poetic flourish about the vast territories and epic voyages that are there to be taken if we are prepared to look within us.

Succinct and eminently wise, his words roared loud and true and slipped somewhere inside me, where they abide to this day. So there I sat, slightly ridiculous in my military fatigues, two paragraphs into my latest travel guide, and three hours away from hauling myself across the frozen wastes of several continents in order to – well, do something I could just as easily have done at home? As the bus coughed into life and we headed for the airport, the ironic timing of this semi-digested insight was not lost upon me.

Modern Era, Ancient Path

Traditionally, the path of mindfulness is understood to be gradual. We progress along it gently and deepen our understanding by degrees. This unhurried process is also true for the historical development of the path, across the continents, from antiquity to our world today.

Relative to its vintage, the huge interest in mindfulness in the West over recent times is as brief as it is exceptional. We live in a time where, from the spiritual fringes to mainstream healthcare, mindfulness-based courses as well as trainings and activities are mushrooming. Mindfulness is now taught regularly in hospitals, clinics and leisure centres, and makes guest appearances in schools, colleges and the boardrooms of the business world.

It was not always so. As the American scientist Jon Kabat-Zinn – a seminal figure in bringing mindfulness into medical settings – has noted, it was barely conceivable until recently that mindfulness would find any substantial role in the Western world. This is despite it being right under the nose of Western civilization for several centuries.

Remembered Words

How did this path arrive on the doorstep of the West? We can retrace steps leading back to the 1960s, when teachers of mindfulness, yoga and other Eastern disciplines first had large-scale contact with subcultures of curious Westerners. It was these Westerners who later brought it to the attention of people in the medical and psychology professions.

We can follow the trail further back in time, to the European explorers of eighteenth- and nineteenth-century colonial India, who initiated a rediscovery of a tradition they would rename 'Buddhism', which had all but died out in its homeland. Through chance detections of long-buried ruins, laborious excavations and the piecemeal deciphering of inscriptions on ancient relics, they wove together a tapestry of irrefutable facts about a distant past. This would initiate a cross-continental exchange of psychological knowledge that continues unabated today.

These colonial adventurers also helped to give flesh and bones to a historical figure who many had, until then, thought a myth. Siddhattha Gotama, also known as 'the Buddha' (an honorific title meaning 'one who is awake'), was an Indian sage who developed and taught a set of practices that support the opening of the human mind and heart to profound truths. He was also the architect of the path of mindfulness – its methods, forms and core techniques – that is available to us today.

Over 25 centuries, his teachings were passed on, first by word of mouth, then in written form, and later translated, reclassified, interpreted and reinterpreted. Sometimes they got lost in the passages of history, and sometimes they were found again. Eventually, they made their way west and into books like this one. Despite these many adaptations, the roots of today's established mindfulness trainings are as coherent and unambiguous as they are old and deep.

> Just so, I saw an ancient path, the ancient road along which the fully awakened ones of old had gone.
>
> THE BUDDHA[27]

A Selfless Path

Still, the path of mindfulness is more mysterious than any timeline might suggest. It would be misleading to equate it solely to the Buddhist tradition. Nor can we locate it specifically to that tradition's founder. The word 'Buddha' is a symbolic term for the perfection of qualities of health, wisdom and benevolence that is the potential of every one of us. Just so, the historical Buddha made no personal claim to the path he discovered. Rather it was something he himself stumbled upon.

He likened his discovery to wandering in a dense jungle and finding an ancient road along which people of old had travelled. This road led to an ancient city, a citadel of all things delightful, where growth and prosperity prevailed and where suffering had no purchase. Metaphor is the only means to expressing the nature of such an 'inner' path of liberation, which belongs to no one, yet is there for each of us to tread, and which bears very tangible fruit.

Lasting Impressions

All that now remains of my own explorations east, apart from a journal, a handful of photos and an apparently indestructible pair of flip-flops, is a hazy collection of mental impressions. Remnants of moments lost in time now whirl and pirouette through my mind like pieces of a tumbling jigsaw.

The peculiar-tasting yogurt salad at 30,000 feet... the old hotelier with the apprentice-son who made tea... long night journeys through snow-speckled mountain passes, cold air fizzing through a window frame, the bounce and shudder of tired limbs on a hard wooden seat... the smell of warm bread in a bustling bazaar... a village track populated by playful, unruly children and a clowder of cats... valleys of woodpiles and haystacks lit by winter sun into radiant oranges and deep blue shadows, plumes of smoke rising from flat-earth roofs into transparent skies... forbidding border posts and barbed-wired checkpoints... weary queues of people under the ticking arm of a customs clock, their echoing voices in a dusk-grey hall... an embroidered mat in a mud-walled tea house, swirls of wood-smoke and dust... sick in a bed in the desolate dormitory of a Salvation Army hostel... blanketed figures huddling around a bus by moonlight, a loading bay of mud and puddles, breath hanging in the air under yellow stars... the clatter and flow of train carriages over hot, boundless plains, scents of jasmine, straw and tobacco smoke... the graceful and unfussy resourcefulness of people living amidst that inhospitable terrain… the almond eyes of a frisky dog one morning by my hut on the edge of a forest… the American guy who leapt excitedly up and down on the bend in the road, shouting, 'You're on the path!'… the odd way the mist would hover over the fields in the morning…

Grasping Water

That's all there is. Perhaps another time would offer other memories but, for now, nothing more arises. Isn't that how it is? All through our lives, things happen to us, within us, around us, and then they are gone, consigned to random recall or full-blown annihilation. Trying to hold on to anything real is like grasping water. And so it goes. As I followed that long-established 'outer' path of Westerners travelling east seeking fulfilment that isn't found there (or at any other dot on a map), something quietly released inside.

My fascination with faraway places, new landscapes and vehicular motion was softening. From my window seat of earthly wanderings, that old fixation with the moving spaces outside – the shifting scenes that flash by, movie-like, before disappearing into oblivion – was remoulded into an investigation of the equally transient and awe-inspiring parallel dimension of inner experience. It was like being granted a lifetime special offer: two journeys for the price of one.

The Doing of Being

Mindfulness is all about coming back to the here and now and being alive to what is happening through the senses. It is about taking time to notice. Taking care of the present in this way often reveals interesting and unexpected things.

To foster an intimacy and familiarity with what is unfolding in body, heart, mind and world is, like any training, a gradual process and best conducted little and often. It's true that we can distinguish 'formal' mindfulness practice (various meditative techniques) from 'informal' practice (intentionally bringing awareness to everyday activities). However, it is wise to bear in mind three things.

First, mindfulness is something you can 'do' all the time. Second, there is no right or wrong way to be mindful. Third, what you are developing are qualities you already possess – you are merely uncovering, empowering and applying them in more potent ways. The gymnasium in which you conduct this training is your moment-to-moment experience.

Remedial Work

Often our minds seem to operate independently of our bodies. Our mind is focused on one thing, while our body is performing an unrelated action. Such is the sheer power of the mind that we can easily slide into its stories, fantasies and ruminations without realizing where we've gone. Next thing we know, we're scratching a foot or reaching for a biscuit. We become a body

> Try to be mindful, and let things take their natural course. Then your mind will become still in any surroundings, like a clear forest pool. All kinds of wonderful, rare animals will come to drink at the pool, and you will clearly see the nature of all things.
>
> FROM 'A STILL FOREST POOL'
> Ajahn Chah (1918–1992)[28]

hanging off the end of a brain. This is no way to be alive to the totality of existence.

To heal the split between the physical and mental takes gentle, persistent effort. Mindfulness practice always begins with attending to bodily experience: physical sensations and the sensory impressions of seeing, hearing, touching, smelling and tasting. This is the gateway to a greater awareness of the workings of self, world and reality. *This* is the means to touching life more fully and gaining more influence over what is on our mind. Developing a taste for relaxing into the present makes for a smoother ride in life.

Back to Basics

The pace of our life is matched only by the speed of our restless and turbulent human mind, which is constantly on the go – frequently unhelpfully so. To reconnect with what is occurring *here* and *now* requires making space in life and restoring a balance between 'doing' and 'being'. Greater ease and joy invariably follow. Here are some of the key ways to cultivate mindfulness throughout the day:

- STOP That's right, just stop. Stop whatever you are doing for one or two minutes. Lay down whatever is in your hand(s). Let go of whatever is on your mind. Let all activity fall away and allow awareness to pour through your physical self. Focus on the stillness of the body.

- MAKE AN INTENTION After a minute or two (or longer if you wish), make a conscious intention to carry on with what you were doing *and* pay attention to what you are doing.

- SLOW DOWN States of mindlessness are characterized by unawareness. Slowing down is a deliberate act that, in itself, helps to break the unpromising trance of automatic behaviour. By slowing down we see more of what is happening, we sharpen awareness and stay in touch with ourselves. The slower you go, the more you will notice.

- DO ONE THING AT A TIME Choose one task and grant yourself permission to forget about the rest. Where possible, mentally 'park' whatever else is on your mind. Approach your chosen activity as something to be experienced rather than ticked off a list. Let go of grasping after future results. Make a virtue out of 'single-tasking'! Take an interest in all the mini-actions that comprise everyday activities, like preparing food, brushing teeth and putting on clothes.

- STAY WITH THE SENSES Our senses are like open doors, always receiving what is coming in from 'outside'. What is in sensory consciousness is what is taking place right now. Paying attention to what is happening – distinct from our interpretations and judgements – allows a fuller, more vital contact with the 'suchness' of a sound, a taste, a visual form.

- CULTIVATE QUIETNESS Set aside short periods of time to reflect. And to digest the impact of activities. Give time to sit, breathe, be still. Tap the multi-dimensional, interconnected nature of existence by listening, inwardly and outwardly. As the poet and mystic Thomas Merton urged, hold yourself so quietly that you can listen to the very stones of the wall.

Dropping Anchor

Mindfulness of breathing is, traditionally, a primary practice. As a resting place, refuge and anchor for attention, the breath is always available. To be aware of one's breathing is to abide at the inter-face of 'inside' and 'outside', change and continuity, being alive and being dead.

Perhaps because it marks the start and end point of our lives, breathing has always fascinated humans. Many ancient cultures – Egyptian, Chinese, Celtic, to name but a few – associated breathing with a sacred and universal life force. The Greek word *psyche* ('soul'), which has its root in the verb *psychein* ('breathe'), points further to veiled connections between the worldly and the spiritual. The Latin word *inspirare* ('breathe in') imports a dual meaning into contemporary

English, for don't we all seek inspiration from this mortal existence that goes beyond the mere intake of oxygen?

Primal Roots

Breathing is a vital function with several unusual aspects. It is available to all the core senses – touch, smell, sound, taste and vision – and to subtler perceptual processes connected to your sense of self. It is synchronized to other vital physical functions and is acutely responsive to the fluctuation of emotional and mental states. Bringing awareness to breathing necessarily locates your experience at the meeting point of mind and body.

The breath is a powerful tool for sharpening, strengthening and refining understanding of the self. To assume the position of a participating observer of one's breath is to gain first-hand experience of the delicate and complex process of who, what and how 'you' are.

There is no right or wrong way to breathe. Nor is mindfulness of breathing something you can master or fail at. It is a way of enquiring into the ebb and flow of moment-to-moment existence and a refuge amidst inevitable change. With practice, mindfulness of breathing reveals a means to both cultivating states of calm and procuring insights about self and reality. These are, by nature, profoundly healing.

JUST BREATHING

- Sit on a chair or cushion in an upright, relaxed posture. Allow the back to be comfortably straight, without straining, and your feet to be on the floor.
- Gently close your eyes and take a few moments to become aware of your whole body – the many, varied sensations of pressure and temperature.
- Take several deep in-breaths, allowing the breath to gently flow out in its own time. Then allow the breath to return to its natural rhythm.
- Allow your attention to gather around the sensations of breathing in the body. The rhythm of the breathing. The flow of air into and out from the body. Allow the attention to gently alight on the breath, like a bee landing on a flower.
- Do not change your breathing in any way or try to control it. Do not imagine it. Simply feel it, moment to moment.
- Wait for the in-breath. Wait for the out-breath. Pay close attention to the whole cycle of breathing.
- Thoughts, sounds, feelings and other phenomena will arise and distract your attention. Just notice them and return your attention to the breath. Do this again and again. Be gentle, patient and firm in returning attention to the breath.
- Let all phenomena come and go in awareness. Your intention is to simply focus on the breath. Allow awareness to be open and inclusive of thoughts, sounds and sensations. Don't chase after them or push them away. Let them arise, stay and pass.
- Simply observe and feel the breath. To be fully present to one breath is enough. To be fully with one breath is to be present.

Rude Awakenings

I made it to the retreat. It was my first taste of intensive mindfulness practice and came with all the major ingredients I have since come to expect from meditation: wonder, contentment, pain, confusion, tranquillity, boredom, doubt, delight, frustration, joy and bemusement, to name but a few.

Over ten long days of what was, essentially, a friendly enquiry into the workings of reality, I learned something about what happens when one waits, watches, listens to, and becomes more intimate with the many forms of existence. Hour upon hour, in stillness and silence, sitting and walking, I watched the frolics and fabrications of my treacherous mind. Often I would get lost in its many stories and sub-plots, or ensnared in thickets of resistance to the pain and tiredness that would come. Sometimes I thought I had died from boredom.

Learning to Listen

At other times, I found an extraordinary freedom. It was as if I could cut through the mental mayhem, the fixations with thoughts, and bypass my own urges to fill mental space with fruitless reactions. At these times, I could simply be *with* experiences, rather than be *in* them. I could come to the broad and present happening of the moment. There I detected a flavour of coolness and ease, which was new to me. I liked the taste of it, only to then discover deeper habits of grasping as I suffocated my own efforts to taste it even more. The whole process was like peeling onion after onion. Letting go of the insatiable demands of mind requires patience and kindness. To this day, it is a work-in-progress for me.

My 'take-home message' from that retreat was one that mindfulness practice regularly confers upon people: 'You are not what you think.' On one level, this might appear elementary. Fully explored, however, it is radically life-changing. To acquire some experiential understanding that you are not your thoughts, nor are you what your thoughts say you are, is the basis for unbinding from all mental suffering. Mindfulness provides a way of reaching and applying this understanding. It's there for the taking. But you've got to put in the practice.

Heart of the Practice

A mindful approach to life is inextricably connected to deep and boundless qualities of the heart. The urge to be on good terms with oneself is an expression of caring that gives rise to kindness and compassion. These in turn support the practice of awareness.

For a moment, probe inwardly and ask yourself why you are reading this book. In fact, why do you do anything that takes time and effort? At its root, any answer will likely have something to do with caring. This is the motivation that underlies the path of mindfulness: the nobility of the human heart to meet the pain of human experience with enduring

THE POWER OF PRACTICE

When I was aged between 18 and 21 and living either on my own or with friends, once a year I would cry suddenly without warning signs (possibly due to unacknowledged accumulated stress or tension) for a whole day. Then the storm would pass and I would be fine again. As soon as I started meditating regularly, as a nun in a Zen Buddhist monastery in Korea, this stopped and it never happened again.

After spending ten years in the monastery, I disrobed and went to live in England. The practice of mindfulness was a great help in adapting to very different circumstances. But one time, in the depths of winter, I woke up feeling low and grey. This lasted for a total of two weeks. Every day I would wake up and the mood was just there – for no apparent reason apart from the weather and the season.

Mindfulness helped me to be aware of the mood without amplifying it or identifying with it. It was there like the rain, happening according to conditions. I did not worry about it; I just let it be while carrying out my various activities. Then one day, I met someone and listened to their difficulties. A great compassion arose in me and the low mood totally dissipated, to be replaced by kindness and love.

This showed me that we can coexist with difficult feelings with the help of mindfulness; then they do not become overwhelming and, in due time, they disappear. From that point on I was no longer afraid of my feelings.

Martine Batchelor
Writer & Meditation Teacher

> Sometimes remembering our basic goodness
> takes a leap of faith. The trick is to connect with
> the soft spot that we already have.
>
> PEMA CHÖDRÖN
> Buddhist teacher & writer[29]

compassion, empathy and patience. It is also the deep longing we feel to rise to the occasion of our own existence.

Unfailingly, we take up mindfulness practice because we care. Knowing places of darkness and suffering, we find in ourselves the capacity to explore and understand them. In so doing, a reciprocal process takes place. We begin to cultivate awareness, and a greater sense of kindness towards ourselves and others arises, in its own way, in its own time. Perhaps it is through waking up to what's happening, to the interconnectedness of life, that such qualities of the heart express themselves more fully while negative, habitual mental reactions begin to diminish. A kindly attitude towards life in turn facilitates an open, receptive awareness. A positive, invigorating energy field quietly begins to generate itself. The unlimited warmth and strength that emerges is a slow-release antidote to the vicious cycles of stress, depression and anxiety.

A Fertile Ground

Awareness is, in itself, transformative. It is receptive, even-handed and non-judgemental in nature. Not only is it cultivated from the same ground as compassion, it also moistens experience in such a way that other, dynamic qualities are brought into being: mental concentration, tranquillity, curiosity, wise discrimination and equanimity. The skills of attentiveness, empathy and a greater capacity to bear life's pains are just some of the helpful by-products that come with opening to the present in an impartial, non-interfering way.

What could be more useful in life than an interest and willingness to embrace whatever is happening? Without that, this insecure and changeable world offers only two possibilities: having experiences we don't want, or not having ones that we do want. Any takers?

Wisdom traditions of all kinds, past and present, tell us the same thing: compassion and kindness are innate conditions of the human heart. In the same way that we don't need to acquire something we call 'mindfulness' from outside of ourselves, there are no qualities of the 'good heart' that are alien to us. These are readily available, in limitless measure, and they spring from within. They are as natural to you as the open palm of your hand – how effortless that is compared to holding a closed fist!

CHAPTER FOUR

Hello Darkness, My Old Friend

Walk any path and obstacles will arise. It is the nature of the world to confront us with the unwanted. A mindful approach to life is about embracing whatever impedes our flow or blocks our way. We reconcile ourselves with the ungainly aspects of reality and, conversely, find a freedom to move beyond them. It is the same when dealing with depression, an obstacle with a tendency to reappear. The arising of depression is an opportunity to make its acquaintance. In fully meeting it, and knowing it, we can step out of its shadow and live in the light.

Learning How to Play the Blues

Mindfulness practice encourages an opening up to what is occurring in the world around us and within us, be that wanted or unwanted. It is about approaching life in a spirit of friendly enquiry. It is not about trying to maintain happy states or about denying what hurts.

This is the radical invitation of mindfulness: to befriend the painful aspects of existence so as to better understand them, and unbind from any struggle with them. This willingness to meet fully with what comes our way is the antithesis of biological drives to destroy or flee from unpleasant experiences. The practice of mindfulness draws as much upon our tolerance and fortitude as our capacity to be kind.

Rather than viewing difficulties as obstructions to what we conceive as 'progress', might it be possible to see them as opportunities in our quest to live more freely? This is the challenge of mindfulness when approaching the 'problem' of depression. A brief consideration of some basic truths about clinical depression suggests the good sense of relating to this common mental state with interest rather than resistance:

1. *It is a time-honoured human experience.*
2. *It can seriously undermine your quality of life.*
3. *Mild or severe, swift or enduring, it is always unpleasant.*
4. *There is no reliable cure for it.*
5. *It has a tendency to return.*

There you have it: five short statements of fact that you probably wish weren't so. And, incidentally, five statements that are also true for many other aspects of human psychology.

Resistance is Futile

It is understandable that depressed states give rise to powerful urges to get rid of or somehow change them – in short, to avoid them. Avoidance is a fundamental human strategy for dealing with uncomfortable situations. It works really well when we are confronted with physical threats; but it fails hopelessly for 'internal' problems like depression because it sets up a painful struggle with subjective experience. At best, attempts to avoid discomfort result in suppression of thoughts and feelings, which only increases inner tension and dis-ease.

In terms of depression, avoidance of 'given experience' is the ground upon which all species of mental negativity grow: the critical commentaries and pervasive judgements; the compulsive focusing on the gap between the way things are and the way we want them to be; the impatient straining to be somewhere else. In our quest to live with greater contentment, avoidance is a non-starter.

Turn On, Tune In, Let Go

Mindfulness, in contrast, offers a means to approaching 'given experience' regardless of whether it is pleasant or unpleasant. It is all about a willingness to experience what is being experienced, and an openness to allowing things to arise and pass away in their own time. Such a stance is the essence of what many wisdom traditions refer to as 'letting go'.

In extending our boundaries of tolerance, we find the capacity to stand steady amidst the storms in our mind. This points to one of the contradictions of awareness practice: it is a 'non-doing' rather than a 'doing'. Existence happens all by itself, as does the awareness of it. All we actually 'do' is keep cultivating the *intention* to remain awake to what is happening. Paradoxically, this facilitates a greater control of the mind.

To work mindfully with depression, then, is to 'lean into' it, to explore its textures and energies and its impact on the mind and heart. Such an attitude eases the inner contractions that constitute depression.

Shaking Hands with Depression

Over the years, the basic components of my depression haven't changed much. My mood drops several degrees below flat, the world appears lifeless, my mind feels like quicksand, and my thoughts play their same old forlorn tunes. Ho-hum. What has transformed – and is transformative – is my relationship to these states.

It used to be that all I wanted was not to be depressed. 'Get me out of this!' was my anguished (usually stifled) cry. But that merely pasted another layer of aversion onto an already hate-filled predicament. I've since learned to become interested in depression. 'What is this thing?' is the rousing enquiry that seems to neutralize the aversion and soothes the aching disparity between what I want and what I've actually got. It's an amiable enquiry that seeks to genuinely know the thin, dark clouds that flit along the edges of awareness.

Friendly Phantasms

Like a charismatic old con man, depression tries to insinuate itself into my world when my back is turned. Perhaps at work, when demands on my inner resources threaten to outstrip their capacity, a mental demon will quietly mount a hostile take-over of my powers of reason. Or lazing on the sofa, tranquillized by gloomy news reports, my mind will conjure an impression of life as perpetual conflict and estrangement. I catch an auto-suggestion that I should save my energy by abandoning all hope.

Even when external conditions are favourable, such as relaxing on holiday, a murkiness may creep between the rays of a bleaching sun to block out the light of my day. Like a nimble street tout who seems to materialize from nowhere to deliver the 'hard sell', the voice of depression catches me unawares with a compact sermon, delivered in the most alluring of tones, on the fragility of joy and good fortune, before making its customary appeal: wouldn't I feel more secure in the comfortable crush of that old black hole?

A Formless Presence

Depression is a master of disguise, but it can be unmasked and known. On first encounter, it may appear static, monotonous and overwhelming, but this changes upon investigation. Its powers of seduction melt under the floodlights of awareness. When fully inspected, I find depression to be changeable and fluid. It might explode into my life as an aftershock from a painful or tragic event, bringing with it a whole retinue of stories about the past and future. It might hover on the peripheries of my mind as a foreboding presence. It might snap at my heels like a vengeful black dog setting me up for a good mauling. However it presents itself, it can be examined, befriended and let go of. When I see depression arise, I see it for what it is: an insubstantial occurrence that comes and goes.

Sublime Contradictions

In embracing depression and not seeking to overcome or diminish it, I have found I experience it less intensely, less protractedly and less frequently. This is the essential paradox of the mindful path: change occurs when we cease striving for it.

Mindfulness practice is about being with 'what is' in such a way that change can unfold organically. This willingness to turn towards *all* experience, including the difficult, and to know it and *feel* it, amounts to a radical acceptance of reality. Acceptance is not resignation or submission; it is an active engagement with life. In terms of unwanted experience, acceptance is about making room for both painful feelings *and* the aversion that arises to them.

WHAT I'VE LEARNED

My mother was my first teacher. She suffered from anxiety-driven depression, for which she took a concoction of prescription drugs. She told me that mothering four children was what kept her going. That was my first lesson: Keep doing what you have to do.

She transformed when with friends. No matter how she felt, she engaged. That was my second lesson: You have to laugh!

These two strategies, I believe, kept me from taking drugs, but did not tackle the root problem, which was my relationship to anxiety and depression. Not until I began to practise mindfulness meditation did the real cure begin.

The Buddha asks us to really challenge painful feelings in a kind, open-hearted way. He instructs us to allow ourselves to open up to our feelings, both physical and emotional, and to fully experience them.

It takes trust to open up. At times we may feel overwhelmed. But should we persist, we will create a different relationship to experience. This is one of radical acceptance: this is the way it is. It is one of equanimity: open-heartedness and open-mindedness. And it is one of fearlessness: patient forbearance and the willingness to bear.

This new relationship, rooted in non-aggression and non-fear, allows something magical to happen. All that oppressive turbulence begins to exhaust itself. It becomes less dense and doesn't persist so long. Inadvertently, we can also find a way not simply to bring depression to an end, but all suffering.

Bhante Bodhidhamma
Buddhist Monk & Meditation Teacher

The Latin root of the word 'acceptance' is *capere*, meaning 'take'. True acceptance is, therefore, 'taking what is offered'. In so doing, a wondrous alchemy takes place. By allowing ourselves to unconditionally 'take in' experience, we generate an internal representation of it that matches what has actually happened. When 'inner' appraisals and 'outer' realities become attuned, they allow a healthy and stress-free processing of life events. Such an alignment of inner and outer is made possible by mindfulness, which contributes that essential ingredient of lucid, steady, even-handed attention.

Magic Ingredients

The link between mindfulness and the 'paradox of change' is tellingly captured in the story of the birth of Mindfulness-Based Cognitive Therapy. MBCT is an eight-week group programme designed to tackle the chronic, repetitive nature of depression. It was devised in the 1990s by psychologists Zindel Segal, Mark Williams and John Teasdale, based on a pioneering format devised by Jon Kabat-Zinn and colleagues two decades earlier.

Initially, Segal, Williams and Teasdale were not interested in the wholesale adoption of mindfulness. Rather they wanted to incorporate the basic skill of 'attentional control' into their fledgling cognitive therapy programme. After their first visit to Kabat-Zinn's Stress Reduction Clinic in Massachusetts to gather ideas, they declined to imbue their project with the spirit of profound, open-hearted, existential enquiry that typifies any authentic mindfulness training. Instead, they devised a programme that partly drew on mindfulness technique but still viewed depression as a problem to be 'fixed'. In live trials, this programme proved to be unworkable.

Uncertain as to how to proceed, the three psychologists returned to Massachusetts, wondering what was amiss with their work. It was only when they looked more closely at what was happening at the Stress Reduction Clinic that they fully grasped the depth and subtlety of mindfulness practice.

The instructors in Massachusetts did not try to fix problems or provide solutions. They encouraged a penetrating investigation of immediate experience with a resolutely welcoming attitude, and that was all. Segal, Williams and Teasdale now discerned more clearly the elegant fusion of radical acceptance and goalless awareness that lay at the heart of mindfulness. This wasn't about trying to alter the difficult, or avoid problems; it was about opening to them and living amidst them. Once they had this kernel of understanding, it fundamentally shifted the way they approached their work. In this way, the attitude of radical acceptance became the foundation stone for MBCT, one of the most inventive and effective mainstream treatments for depression in modern times.

Unravelling Confusion

Mindfulness practice is often misunderstood as an endeavour to achieve a particular state, be a certain way, stop thinking, or somehow 'space out'. This is symptomatic of wider misconceptions about the nature of meditation, which is the principal vehicle for cultivating mindfulness.

Written words cannot convey the experience of meditation, but they can clarify something of its purpose and function. Mindfulness meditation is the formal practice of observing how the mind behaves. It is also about learning how to make a gentle shift from the mind's automatic reactions to a more deliberate 'holding in mind' of psycho-physical phenomena as they arise and pass away. This allows us to respond more wisely and compassionately to what is going on in our lives.

Undoing the Knots

Using awareness of the body, we learn to tune into sensory experience. This aids clearer and quicker perception of the changing feeling-tones – pleasant, unpleasant, neutral – of experience. These feeling-tones normally activate spontaneous, involuntary reactions. But with steady attention and bright, receptive awareness, it becomes possible to detect these more quickly, along with other mental obscurations, and engage wisely with them rather than react unwittingly. With patience and care, we begin to disentangle the bare elements of experience from the mental 'story' we build around them.

It is deeply liberating to be freed from the distortions of the mind – its incessant comparing, judging and fantasizing – and the mental proliferations they condition. Rather than feeling like a ball bearing bouncing around a pinball machine, we acquire a centredness and inner agency. This is particularly helpful if we are prone to depression because it leaves us better equipped to deal with a principal feature of all depressions: negative thinking.

Propaganda of the Mind

In the same way that fish are unaware they exist in water, humans are commonly oblivious to being enveloped in thought. We fail to see what's right under our nose: the rapid, automatic, fleeting, habitual flow of thoughts that pervade and inform our subjective world.

Thinking is, of course, an essential part of life. We need to be able to analyse, evaluate, imagine, plan, reflect and perform various mental acrobatics in order to live our lives. It is easy to take these skills for granted. And it is even easier to assume that it's we who are always in charge of our thoughts. Mindfulness practice reveals a very different psychological reality.

Through awareness, we begin to see how much of our thinking is not conscious, intentional or rational. Rather, it is our thoughts that drive us, influencing our actions and reactions, and holding sway over our moods and emotions. The more we investigate, the more we discover how much the thinking mind has a life of its own.

> When the mind is thinking, it is talking to itself.
>
> PLATO (FIFTH CENTURY BCE)
> Philosopher

To observe this process in action is a wonder. Meditating, we begin to get a peek at how the mind fashions its own reality in the same way the brain generates a mental representation of everything physical in the world 'out there'. Instead of being trapped in the mind, hauled from one emotional dragnet to the next like characters in a soap opera, we can sit back, watch the show and appreciate it for what it is.

Thought Control

The importance of seeing thoughts for what they are – transitory mental events – is a principal reason for using mindfulness to deal with depression. Such is the nature of the virtual reality generated by our minds that, at the best of times, thinking is arbitrary and biased. When depressed, however, this is blown out of all proportion. The depressed mind routinely ignores, dismisses and filters out anything contrary to its view of life as a joyless and deadening affair. Life is interpreted in the negative by a mind that is attracted to the bleak expanses of hate, blame and hopelessness. The swirling and brooding nature of depressed thinking obscures awareness of the vivid, changing present. Virtual reality takes the form of a virtual hell.

If left unexamined – that is, outside of awareness – the thinking patterns that fuel depression become the dormant seeds for future suffering. Depression is recurrent. The likelihood of you being depressed in the future increases with each episode of depression. This is because people with a history of depression are more likely to experience already established negative thinking patterns in any period of low mood, no matter how mild. The resulting interplay between negative thinking and low mood can trigger a decline into depression.

Mindfulness helps to arrest this downward spiral by facilitating greater clarity about *what is actually going on*. By grounding awareness in the body and assuming a position of affectionate curiosity, we can observe the rippling currents of mental propaganda and unpleasant feelings that normally hijack us. We find a sense of distance and space in relation to these objects of awareness. Negative mental patterns are drained of their energy and begin to lose their sting.

In embracing the present in all its aspects, we can drop the struggle with internal pain. This grants us a fresh perspective on life – one offering greater choice as to what happens next.

JUST THINKING

- Sit in an upright and relaxed posture. Allow the body to become still. Close your eyes. Take a few moments to focus your attention on the sensations of breathing in the body.
- Now deliberately bring full awareness to what is happening in the mind. Simply watch what it does.
- Wait for thoughts, images and mental impressions to appear. Observe them with interest but without interference. Don't try to change, influence or censor anything. Just observe.
- If no thoughts or images appear, simply notice their absence. Sooner or later, some kind of mental impression will arise.
- Observe all the contents of the mind keenly, just as a wildlife enthusiast might watch wildlife from a hide on a nature reserve – intently, objectively and without intruding.
- Observe, as best you can, all the contents of the mind as they come and go. Treat every thought, image and mental impression the same. Do not chase or hold on to anything. Remain an impartial witness to what is happening.
- It's normal to get lost in thoughts. When you realize you've lost the 'position' of pure observer and have become caught up in thoughts, or that you are thinking about your thoughts (!), relax. Bring your attention to the sensations of breathing in the body. Fully experience one or two breaths as a way of re-establishing a clear intention of 'just noticing', then again assume the position of observing the mind.
- Every time you get 'caught up' in the contents of the mind, or get distracted from observing the mind, briefly bring your attention back to the breath and then start again.

Going Deeper

On my early meanderings on the path, I developed an eagerness for formal practice and a trust in its potential to precipitate greater contentment and insight. Equally useful were the many, often painful lessons I learned about the fickle nature of the mind and the delicate art of taming it.

One occasion stands out. I had signed myself up to undertake a solo, intensive, two-week retreat with a Burmese teacher who ran a small retreat centre in a remote suburb of Kathmandu. By this time, I had attended several retreats – sometimes practising for up to 14 hours a day – and had acquired an ease and familiarity with mindfulness. I thought I knew a thing or two. I turned up, brimming with self-assurance, expecting to be 'enlightened' within the fortnight.

No Way Out

By lunchtime on the first day, I was reduced to a wreck. Assailed by loneliness, fear and doubt, I was horrified at the velocity of my feral mind and overwhelmed by my resistance to the prospect of spending hour upon hour, day upon day, exploring the minutiae of each moment. Come the afternoon, I was virtually pleading with the teacher to let me clear weeds, clean windows, scrub floors, do *anything* as a distraction from the interminable weight of existence. Given that I had chosen to do this retreat and had staked a high value on it, I felt like a failure. All possibilities of a fulfilled life seemed lost to my despairing mind. The clouds of depression gathered. I wondered if mindfulness practice had a dark side.

Caught in the Undercurrents

In an interview later that day, after patiently listening to my outpourings of misery, the teacher smiled softly and said: 'This is not a jail.' It seemed obvious but I was grateful for the reminder. He continued in broken English: 'When you practise meditation, only present moment useful. Past, future, both useless. Useless. So relax. Keep practice simple.' Like all good teachings, it was simple and encouraging. I resolved to stick out the retreat. It proved to be one of the most fruitful I've ever undertaken, mainly because of the wealth of experience I garnered in the workings of my maddening mind.

It transpired that the 'dark side' I had mused about was something I'd brought upon myself – something my mind was adept at – namely 'grasping'. Mental grasping is the deeply conditioned habit of wanting something different from what is happening. It is the instinctive smash-and-grab of the mind – its tendency to cling to pleasant experiences and to reject unpleasant ones without reflection. Grasping is the antecedent for all the seeking more of, and less of, that we unconsciously do in life. It is the fathomless root of all our attempts to control experience in this world of uncontrollable change.

The retreat was an enduring lesson in the power of my mind to lead itself down dead ends. Such is the forgiving nature of mindfulness that, over the years, this and many other of my blunders on the path have turned out to be blessings in disguise.

Removing the Sting

The deliberate simplifying and steadying of attention that characterizes awareness practice is what allows a clearer understanding of the primitive play of the mind. This can be an alarming wake-up call, but practice is nothing more than an encounter with the mental hustle and bustle that is already happening inside your head.

Giving space to this inner clamour and 'letting go' are the antidotes to grasping. With gentle and consistent effort, the mind becomes more malleable and stops careening so wildly back and forth between indulgence and rejection. Its blind reactivity subsides and it learns to relax with what comes along, without picking and choosing. Judgements, resistance and impatience drop away. The mind calms and settles. As it does so, a deeper immersion takes place. The mind begins to know itself more clearly.

It is possible to observe, at first hand, the effects of grasping. Grasping is rooted in an ongoing and unrealistic attempt to fix circumstances in ways continually favourable to the self. But circumstances are fluid and unreliable, and so grasping only compounds pain and enhances the self's sense of lack. The result is magnified unpleasantness and the triggering of more distress. In understanding grasping, a releasing from it takes place organically.

Two Darts

Life is a pain in the sense that uncomfortable and unwanted experiences happen. But our reaction to these experiences is optional. If we react with aversion, then we will lament, berate and ruminate. If our reaction is one of opening to and abiding with, then we will not experience all the secondary pain that flows in the wake of aversion. Instead, we will discover a flexibility to engage with what is coming our way.

This is a paraphrasing of the Buddha's simile of the two darts. The simile describes the experience of a man who is hit by a dart and feels physical pain. This first dart is a reference to the fact of existential discomfort. The simile then goes on to describe how, if the man is unmindful, it is as if he is struck by a second dart. This second dart is the man's own aversive mental reaction to the first. It takes the form of worry, resentment or distress about the first dart. This aversive reaction is optional – the man brings it upon himself. Conversely, says the Buddha, one who is well-practised in mindfulness simply does not experience this second dart and, by extension, all the emotional pain and stress that it conveys.

Depression can be understood as one expression of the second dart. The inevitable pains, losses and dissatisfactions that life throws our way are the first darts. The resistance to these, our broodings over them, and our efforts to get away from them are the second darts. The second darts are the ones we throw at ourselves. But in 'waking up' to the nature of life, we learn a more skilful relationship to it and let go of the pain we bring upon ourselves. Suffering abates when we stop throwing darts. It's that simple.

Meeting Your Demons

Roads develop potholes and lose their markings. Tracks become overgrown and flood. Passageways get clogged with junk and detritus. And so it is that any path we may tread in life will encounter a number of pitfalls, obstructions and hazards. The path of mindfulness is no different.

Training in mindfulness can be an unsettling encounter with mental habits that stifle us and create suffering. One moment we may be abiding in a calm, alert contemplation only to be 'swept away' in the next, plunged headlong into some random fantasy, hooked up in an irritating memory or worry, or submerged by a wave of drowsiness or agitation.

Such entanglements are just the mind's tendency to impede our best efforts to live with fluency and ease. It is the nature of the mind to ambush one's intentions to live wakefully.

The Great Destroyer

Like any aspect of given experience, powerful psychological forces that block or mislead can be known and befriended. It is useful to understand something of how they operate. Traditional teachings on what we call 'devils' offer clues here. The word 'devil' comes from the Greek *diabolos* meaning 'to hurl across (a path)'. Synonymous terms are the Hebrew word Satan, meaning 'opposer', and the Arabic word Shaitan, meaning 'that which leads astray'. The common connection between all of these terms is of an adversarial force that confronts, obstructs and deludes.

Devils are compelling metaphors for what stop us in our tracks – the habitual patterns and traits within us, which work against our well-being. The mythological figure I am most familiar with is Mara, the devil of Buddhist cosmology, a god of once good standing who uses his power to a perverted end. He is the embodiment of everything that constricts any effort to live wisely. He plays many parts: killer, trickster, flatterer, critic, seducer, deluder. He is never far away because he is nothing more than an aspect of the ordinary human mind.

Devil in the Detail

In psychological terms, Mara represents the 'hindrances' of sensual desire, ill will, restlessness, dullness and drowsiness, and doubt. These are features of the mind that disturb and obscure inner clarity. Like Mara, they may take many forms, coarse and subtle. With mindfulness, they can be noted either as topics that frequent the mind or energies that frequent the body. They might arise in singular forms, such as the commitment-phobic dithering that is doubt. Aternatively, they might arise in mixed forms. One example of this is boredom, which is a combination of dullness, ill will and the craving for sensual stimulation.

Instead of wishing away these hindrances, they need to be welcomed with curiosity. They are part of our consciousness and grist to the mill of mindfulness practice. Encountering a hindrance is an indication that there is some form of grasping at work. It is also a sign that the mind is bringing to light an unskilful habit. As this happens, the hindrance will lose its potency. Awareness, after all, is transformative.

Walking the Line

Under the microscope of mindfulness, what we might routinely label our familiar black dog can be deconstructed into its component parts and examined for what they are. Your depression could be any blend of all five hindrances. It will invariably have some measure of discontentment, hostility, inertia, dullness, rigidity, worry, unease and vacillation.

In seeing depression for what it is, transformation becomes possible. The gaze of mindfulness is kindly and bold, and it penetrates to the heart of existence in the most beneficial of ways. Walking this path is about making peace with your inner demons, politely declining their unpromising invitations, and patiently stepping forth in the world.

CHAPTER FIVE

Signposts for the Way Ahead

The path of mindfulness leads us back to where we started: the ordinary and immediate experience of being in the world. There never was anywhere else to go. The revolutionary change that takes place along the way is acquiring the facility to be on wholly good terms with oneself. Peace of mind comes through making peace with the mind. With gentle, consistent effort, one's life and one's practice entwine, offering a refuge from the hard edges and unhelpful habits we encounter in ourselves.

The Journey Home

Sometimes we need to go to the other side of the planet to find something we already have. Sometimes we need to go to the depths of despair to find our true worth. Ultimately, we always have to 'come home' to life as it is, here and now.

Mindfulness practice teaches us to deal with this often troublesome mind, body and world so that we can handle them skilfully. We do this by attending to the ordinariness of each moment. We 'get real' with the ordinary. Through this, a quiet and miraculous adjustment takes place: the ordinary becomes more ordinary than ordinary. It becomes extra-ordinary.

No words can convey the true nature of reality or our direct experience of it. In the language of the Buddha, the term was *tathata*, meaning 'suchness' or 'thusness'. This denotes a state of totality, of being utterly present, of being attuned to the vibrant occurrence of now. The practice of mindfulness offers us the potential of savouring this singularity we call 'the present', which is beyond thought and beyond all conceptions of good and bad, self and other, emptiness and fullness.

A Place of Safety

Our capacity to be awake to the present also offers a sanctuary amidst unreliable and changing conditions. We find a secure base from which to negotiate the vicissitudes of life without identifying with them or denying their existence. When we come back to the here and now – the still point at the centre of our lives – we are able to respond with wisdom rather than react out of ignorance.

Mindfulness practice is, in this sense, about taking refuge in awareness. Taking refuge is something we each do, in multiple ways, consciously and unconsciously. A refuge can be anything that offers dependable shelter and support, such as people, places, objects, ideals and traditions. The path of mindfulness enjoins us to dwell in the clear knowing of the flow of momentary existence – the ground that life perpetually springs from and returns to. This is a refuge that is profound yet elementary. It is one that remains resolutely undisturbed while conditions change, as is their nature, from bitter to sweet, easy to difficult, light to dark. It is one that is equanimous to all that arises and passes away. It is one that is always available since it is indivisible from our being.

Going Native

When I returned to Britain from my forays on foreign trails, I brought with me new knowledge of local places that formally supported mindfulness-based practices. It was a real joy to discover, close to home, worldly refuges – practice groups, retreat centres, monasteries – dedicated to living wakefully. This was significant not just for practical and social reasons, but for personal ones too.

I realized, for the first time, a more substantial and heartfelt homeliness both within myself and on my native turf. My wide-angled quest for a viable way to live well had seen me shift from desperate roadrunner to immobile navel-gazer in far-flung meditation halls, only to finish up back where I started, discovering that what I'd been looking for had been here, waiting, all the while. I now discerned how the signposts along my journey had all been gently directing me to a secure abode – an ancient path with materially existing forms – which I hadn't noticed before, not because it was remote but because it was so close.

Later, some friends and I took the opportunity to set up a meditation centre in England. This was a further expression of manifesting something of great value to us. We had all chanced upon the path of mindfulness in the East but had taken to heart its injunction to live and breathe it, rather than treat it as some exotic flower. So we took some old roots from abroad and planted them on home soil. Like others before us, it was a commonsensical way of bringing the path directly to our own front door. It is in the mundane, day-to-dayness of existence where we need to live with awareness. The key for each of us is to find whatever will best support that effort.

Path of Kindfulness

Awareness practice is nourished and sustained by its warm embrace of the phenomenal world. This warmth is the radiant, expansive emotion of unconditional friendliness that recognizes our innate connection to all living beings. It is an active energy, deep in our interior, and it informs each step on the path.

Sometimes mindfulness is misunderstood as being concerned solely with one's personal mental development. It is rather more a practice of the heart, one that is underpinned by a generosity of spirit and a kindly attention. When we come to view experience as psycho-physical events that come and go by themselves, we cease to develop an identity out of them. Our self-centredness begins to diminish and the petty preoccupations of the untrained mind fall away. In this way, simply paying attention allows us to become more sensitized to the interconnectedness of life. We discover a deeper kinship with other beings, each of whom seeks happiness just as we do. Seeing and feeling this lack of separation between self and others naturally gives rise to a benevolent attitude.

Ethical Dimensions

The effects of practising mindfulness are not confined to subjective experience. The qualities of tolerance and acceptance we bring to our inner life also flow outwards into the world as implicit acts of kindness and non-harming. Mindfulness has a social as well as an individual value. It gives rise to a clearer sense of cause and effect – how our actions in the world lead to particular results, both for our own minds and for the lives of others. As we become more attuned to these effects, we learn to act more skilfully.

In this way, mindfulness fosters a commitment to ethical integrity. In the Buddhist tradition, conducting one's life in a resolutely mindful fashion is described by the word *appamada*, which means 'heedfulness'. Here we find the explicit connection between a person's mindfulness and the ways in which their care and circumspection impact on the world around them. The 'inner' and 'outer' dimensions of experience are umbilically linked through one's actions. Understanding this allows a person to engage more appropriately and creatively with the world. Mindfulness, therefore, engenders responsibility – not just in terms of one's sense of accountability, but also one's response-ability.

Befriending the Blue Meanies

The warm heart of mindfulness is where our own emotional well-being is fully actualized. We learn to connect more deeply with ourselves as well as with others. Kindly awareness is the necessary antidote for all mind states characterized by a chief feature of most depressions: self-criticism.

Rejection or disapproval of oneself can take many forms. There are all those petty little slights, when we quietly tell ourselves we shouldn't be feeling how we are feeling. And then there are the wholesale annihilations of everything we are and ever have been, and the indiscriminate mental labelling of 'I am bad/not good enough/useless/unworthy' that usually accompanies them. What all varieties of self-condemnation precipitate are emotional states such as anger and fear and contractions within the body. These solidify the sense of a separate self, stifle interest and cut us off from a wider connection with humanity.

This process reminds me of a scene from the 1960s animated film *Yellow Submarine*, based around music by The Beatles. In it, the merry, colourful, music-loving world of Pepperland is subject to a gratuitous attack by the Blue Meanies, a species of demented killjoys and buffoons. The Blue Meanies' combined weaponry has the effect of petrifying the Pepperlanders, reducing them to statues and draining them of colour. Their world fades to a stale grey and the music stops. This is a fitting metaphor for the oppressive effects of self-attacking, when we become immobilized under the barrage of our own negativity. Playfulness, curiosity and creative expression are killed off by the mental projectiles we throw. We become a Blue Meanie to ourselves, bent on committing acts of self-sabotage. In so doing, we find ourselves born into a static and loveless domain.

All You Need is Love

Kindness will melt the absurd cruelty of self-persecution. If we hate ourselves, we simply strengthen aversion and ill will. If we offer ourselves goodwill, we are no longer fighting an internal battle, and we allow positive change to take place. By embracing all parts of ourselves with warm attention and interest, we loosen emotional knots and give our faults space to transform themselves. Mindfulness practice goes hand in hand with unconditional friendliness – our natural capacity for love. This is not a sentimental or sensual love, but the courageous opening of the heart to the entirety of life. It is this

> Great fullness of being, which we experience as happiness, can also be described as love. To be undivided and unfragmented, to be completely present, is to love. To pay attention is to love.
>
> FROM 'LOVING-KINDNESS'
> Sharon Salzberg[30]

that enables us to step out of the barren shadows of self-absorption and negativity, and fully connect with ourselves and the world.

Traditionally, mindfulness meditation is complemented by a second formal practice of cultivating goodwill. This involves empowering intentions of friendliness towards ourselves and others. In meditation, good wishes are offered, such as: 'May I be safe, well and happy; may others be safe, well and happy.' These are extended impartially, without limit or prejudice, from an open heart. Such a practice helps to support an attitude of benevolence to all beings and enliven actions reflecting this. It is also a powerful means to 'holding in mind' the spirit of radical acceptance that informs any and all efforts to live with awareness. The path of mindfulness emerges from, and leads back into, an ocean of kindness.

JUST WALKING

- Take a walk for the experience of walking. Perhaps around a park or any quiet, open space. Rather than needing to get somewhere, use this time as a break from having to 'do' anything.
- Walk naturally. The only difference to how you normally walk is that you are deliberately applying your mind to what you are doing *as* you are doing it.
- Adjust your pace to suit your state of mind. Walk faster if drowsy or if there is a lot of thinking. Walk slower if you feel restless or irritable. Gaze softly ahead.
- As you take each step, tune into the sensations that accompany the motion of the body. Give particular attention to the contact between the soles of the feet and the ground. Use this contact point as a way of anchoring yourself in the present. Allow awareness to inhabit the body and senses.
- Notice each step. Notice the changing pattern of physical sensations in the legs and feet as they alternately receive the weight of the body. Relax. Let go of any concepts about walking. Let the body walk itself. Walking is automatic. It doesn't require thought. It just happens. Let it just happen.
- Distractions will arise. The mind will get caught up in chains of thoughts, sounds or visual phenomena. This is normal. As soon as you realize the mind has wandered, gently and patiently escort the attention back to the sensations of contact between the feet and the ground.
- Don't expect the mind to be still. Allow whatever arises in the mind to pass through. Stay with the experience of walking, the sensations of touch and movement.

Markers on the Road

The path of mindfulness bridges the deep ravines and chasms of depression. It offers a sure footing amidst the weightless places that cut the human heart cold with fear and despair. If followed, it leads still further to a profound contentment and fulfilment in life. These rewards come only with practice.

This whole book is, essentially, a signpost. It points to a path, which you must find and walk for yourself, if you so choose. It is not enough to read books. You must practise and find your own way. This takes effort but, in time, trust develops and the effort becomes effortless. Mindfulness is infinitely supportive, gentle and forgiving once you bring it into your life. It becomes possible to live and act with ease in the world, and to transform one's experience of oneself in the process. Change is often very quiet.

Know For Yourself

It is important to bear in mind that mindfulness is a quality that can be cultivated at any time and in many ways. You don't need to look outside of yourself to acquire it. You've already got it. The exercises in this book will hopefully aid you in this regard. The skill lies in being sensitive to the conditions that best support your efforts to live with greater calm and awareness. These will vary depending on your current circumstances. For example, it is generally not advisable, if in the midst of a depressive episode, to embark on an in-depth programme

> Do not go upon what has been acquired by repeated hearing, by tradition, by rumour, by scripture, by conjecture, by inference, or by product of mere reasoning, or because it conforms with one's preconceived notions, or because it is authoritative, or because of the status of your teacher...
> Know for yourself.
>
> THE BUDDHA[31]

of meditation. Nor is mindfulness necessarily a good substitute for resolving personal issues that could be better explored with a counsellor or psychotherapist.

It is for you to know and find out what is the most useful next step. The foundational teachings of mindfulness encourage self-reliance and rigorous personal assessment. The path must be tested and its usefulness discerned for oneself.

Vital Signs

Establishing a mindfulness practice is a very personal undertaking, influenced by factors such as prior experience, current lifestyle and levels of practical support. In the West today, training programmes are flourishing and opportunities for practice – individual and collective – are considerable. If this is new territory to you, here are some guidelines which may help you strike a healthy balance between inner reserves and outer resources:

- **PRACTICE** Developing a regular meditation practice is the surest way of maintaining mindfulness in daily life. The energy and discipline that comes from formal practice is what invigorates bright awareness of moment-to-moment experience and undermines the unconscious influence of negative mental habits. Ten minutes of formal practice every day is more useful than an hour's practice once a week.
- **TRAINING** It is possible to learn and practise by oneself – good literature and functional online materials exist – but most people find they need a robust formal training to sustain them in the long term. Well-established programmes, such as Mindfulness-Based Cognitive Therapy and Mindfulness-Based Stress Reduction, offer sound structures in which to fully develop your practice. Other reputable models, such as Acceptance and Commitment Therapy, provide imaginative and practical methods for incorporating mindfulness into daily life. Another route, much longer established, is through mindfulness groups and centres rooted in one or another of the practice schools of Buddhism.
- **COMMUNITY** Part of the existential human condition is the need to belong. Support and encouragement from like-minded people is a foundation stone of all inner paths. On a purely pragmatic level, practising meditation with others is a strong motivator. Investigating local groups is also a great opportunity to practise open-minded curiosity and discernment. Thoroughly checking out who and what you are getting involved with is crucial. No authentic mindfulness group, trainer or tradition will ever try to coerce, exploit or indoctrinate you.

- TIME Finding a dynamic harmony between 'doing' and 'non-doing' is a skilful means to wise practice. Life abounds with transitions. Each is an opportunity to create space amidst the stream of events. It takes only a minute to relax, breathe, take stock and re-establish a baseline of equanimity before establishing a new intention to act. Be mindful of excessive busyness. Ask yourself: What am I doing that is extra? Direct this question not just to outer activities, but to the contents of your mind and the muscles in your body. Let go. Tune back into the inner silence from which all your doings emerge.
- EFFORT A gentle, patient effort empowers one's practice. On a micro level, it is no more and no less than the energy required to wake up to what is occurring in the here and now. On a macro level, it has four aspects: to sustain positive states that have already arisen; to arouse positive states that have not yet arisen; to abandon negative states once they have arisen; to guard against negative states so that they do not arise. These are traditionally known as the Four Great Efforts. To aid application, they can be distilled down into four questions:

1. *What is beneficial and worth maintaining?*
2. *What is beneficial and worth developing or strengthening?*
3. *What is not beneficial and needs changing?*
4. *What is not beneficial and needs avoiding?*

Reflecting on these questions on a regular basis, and honing your intentions accordingly, offers a sure-fire route to clarity and composure in daily life.

Meeting the World

How easy it is to live in one's own shadow. How simple it is to step out of it. Every moment brings an opportunity for the subtlest of shifts, just enough to let in the light. Through awareness, transformation becomes possible.

This is the real meaning of 'practice': interacting creatively and consciously with the ebb and flow of this ephemeral world. How we speak, how we act and how we move matters. Where we place our attention matters. This moment matters. It's all about the small stuff.

There is no denying the depressions and dark places of life. They are unavoidable and they hurt. But might we discover more about ourselves from immersions in suffering than from the times when all is sweet and comfortable? Depression is a stimulant for change. It is an injunction to look at what we might be overlooking. It asks to be known, understood and let go of. In so doing, we can move beyond it.

Leaning into the Future

Every moment offers potential. The future is unwritten. The world lies at your feet, awaiting your next move. Notice how you can make a choice, right now, to pause reading and focus your attention on something else. Notice how you can choose to move some part of your body or put this book down and start a different activity. Notice how you might choose to decline that suggestion and carry on reading. Whatever you do, it's your choice.

Life is continually seeking a response. Being aware of how you respond in the moment is a gateway to greater freedom. Fully present, you come to a broad, deep understanding of how to engage well with this intricate dance of forms and feelings. Wherever your path next takes you, may it be a step towards whatever is rich and meaningful for you. May you find lasting contentment and ease, and may you encounter the sublime silences, nameless joys and great mysteries of being that lie beyond words.

Endnotes

1. 'A Depression' Collected Poems by Elizabeth Jennings, p91–2 (Carcanet Press, Manchester, UK, 1986). Permission granted.
2. Quoted in *Touched with Fire: Manic-Depressive Illness and the Artistic Temperament* by Kay Redfield Jamison, p19 (Free Press/Simon & Schuster, New York, 1993)
3. 'Inferno', *Divine Comedy* by Dante Alighieri (14th century)
4. *Care of the Soul* by Thomas Moore, p138 (Piatkus, London, 1992)
5. 'After Great Pain A Formal Feeling Comes', *The Poems of Emily Dickinson* edited by Thomas H. Johnson (Belknap/Harvard University Press, Cambridge, Massachusetts, USA, 1955)
6. The Apocrypha, The King James Bible (Oxford University Press, Oxford, UK, 1997)
7. *A Blue Fire: The Essential James Hillman* by James Hillman, p153 (Routledge, London, 1998)
8. 'Black Hole' by William Hammett, copyright 2011.
9. *The Consolation of Philosophy* by Boethius, p58 (The Folio Society/Penguin, 1998)
10. 'Dark Night of the Soul' by Saint John of the Cross, translated by A.Z. Foreman. Online at http://poemsintranslation.blogspot.co.uk/2009/09/saint-john-of-cross-dark-night-of-soul.html
11. *Overcoming Depression*, 3rd edition, by Paul Gilbert, p43 (Robinson, London, 2009)
12. *Overcoming Depression*, 3rd edition, by Paul Gilbert, p20 (Robinson, London, 2009)
13. *A Blue Fire: The Essential James Hillman* by James Hillman, p158 (Routledge, London, 1998)
14. *Franz Kafka: A Biography* by Max Brod, trans. G.H. Roberts and R. Winston (Schocken, New York, 1960)
15. *Sunbathing in the Rain* by Gwyneth Lewis, p135 (Flamingo/Harper Collins, London, 2002)

16. 'What is the best dose of nature and green exercise for mental health? A meta-study analysis.' by J. Barton and J. Pretty, University of Essex, 2010 (quoted in 'Green exercise quickly boosts mental health', BBC News website, 1 May 2010)
17. 'Return to Tipasa' (1952) by Albert Camus, translated in *The Unquiet Vision: Mirrors of Man in Existentialism* by Nathan A. Scott, p116 (World Publishing Co, New York, 1969)
18. *Buddha's Brain: The Practical Neuroscience of Happiness, Love and Wisdom* by Rick Hanson and Richard Mendius, p68 (New Harbinger, Oakland, USA, 2009)
19. *Buddha's Brain: The Practical Neuroscience of Happiness, Love and Wisdom* by Rick Hanson and Richard Mendius, p69 (New Harbinger, Oakland, USA, 2009)
20. *Buddha's Brain: The Practical Neuroscience of Happiness, Love and Wisdom* by Rick Hanson and Richard Mendius, p69 (New Harbinger, Oakland, USA, 2009)
21. *Quotations for Our Time* compiled by Laurence J. Peter, p234 (Magnum, London, 1980)
22. *Living with the Devil: A Meditation on Good and Evil* by Stephen Batchelor, p75 (Riverhead, New York, 2004)
23. *Living with the Devil: A Meditation on Good and Evil* by Stephen Batchelor, p79 (Riverhead, New York, 2004)
24. *Living with the Devil: A Meditation on Good and Evil* by Stephen Batchelor, p77 (Riverhead, New York, 2004)
25. *Man's Search for Meaning* by Viktor E. Frankl, p117 (Rider Books, London, 2004)
26. *Dhammapada* ('Verses on the Eternal Truth'), verse 122, Pali Canon
27. 'The City', *Samyutta Nikaya* ('Connected Discourses') part 2 chapter 1.7, Pali Canon
28. *A Still Forest Pool: The Insight Meditation of Ajahn Chah* edited by Jack Kornfield and Paul Breiter, p162 (Theosophical Publishing House, Illinois, USA, 1985)

29. *The Places That Scare You: A Guide to Fearlessness in Difficult Times* by Pema Chödrön, p85 (Shambhala, Boston, USA, 2002)
30. *Loving-Kindness: The Revolutionary Art of Happiness* by Sharon Salzberg, p15 (Shambhala, Boston & London, 1997)
31. 'The Instruction to the Kalamas', *Anguttara Nikaya* ('Book of Numerical Discourses'), Book of Threes discourse 65, Pali Canon

Index

Abraham 20
acceptance 106
Acceptance and Commitment
   Therapy 134
Alexander the Great 19
anger 15, 32, 33–4
appamada 127
Archimedes 8–9
attention 78–81
avoidance 103
awareness 75–6, 78–9, 82, 94, 97–8, 104

Batchelor, Martine 97
Batchelor, Stephen 65, 67
Baudelaire, Charles 19
Berlioz, Hector 17–18
Bible, the 19
black dogs 21–4
black holes 24–7
Bodhidhamma, Bhante 107
Boethius 28
breathing 92–4
Buddha and Buddhism 69, 77, 86, 107, 120, 124, 127, 133, 134

Camus, Albert 19, 53
Chah, Ajahn 90
changing depressive behaviour 46–51
Chödrön, Pema 98
Churchill, Winston 21
Clangers, The 78
confusion 42–4, 109–13
counselling 39

Dante Alighieri 18
Darwin, Charles 19
demons, meeting 119–21

depression (definition) 14–20
Dickinson, Emily 18
Drake, Nick: *Black-Eyed Dog* 21

Einstein, Albert 46
Elgar, Edward 19
Elijah 19
evolution and depression 29-34
exercises
   From Here to Where? 64
   Identifying Your Dark
      Companion 22
   A Journey in Space 56
   Just Breathing 94
   Just Standing 74
   Just Thinking 114
   Just Walking 131
   Tea Meditation 80

Four Great Efforts 135
Frankl, Viktor E. 68
Freud, Sigmund 19, 34
From Here to Where? 64

Gauguin, Paul 19
Gilbert, Paul 31
green spaces 50
guidelines for mindfulness 133–5

Hammett, William 25
Handel, George Frideric 19
Hanson, Rick 54–5
Hillman, James 24, 32
Hippocrates 21

Identifying Your Dark Companion 22
inner work, importance of 61

Jennings, Elizabeth 116
Jeremiah 20
Job 20
John of the Cross, Saint: *Dark Night of the Soul* 28
Jonah 20
A Journey in Space 56
Just Breathing 94
Just Standing 74
Just Thinking 114
Just Walking 131

Kabat-Zinn, Jon 84, 108
Kafka, Franz 32–3
kindness 126–31

'letting go' 103, 117
Lewis, Gwyneth 39, 47
loss 37

Mara (deity) 120
MBCT *see* Mindfulness-Based Cognitive Therapy
melancholia 20–1
Mendius, Richard 55
mental grasping 116–21
mindfulness
   definition 46, 76–7
   guidelines for 133–5
   key ways to cultivate 90–2
Mindfulness-Based Cognitive Therapy (MBCT) 108, 134
Mindfulness-Based Stress Reduction 134
mindlessness 78–9

negative evaluations 53–4
past, processing the 39–40
path, establishing a 63–6

Plato 112
positivity
   cultivating 55–7
   positive evaluations 53–4
practicing meditation 134
psychotherapy 39–40

rest, importance of 57
rumination 33
Runbeck, Margaret Lee 59

Salzberg, Sharon 130
Satan 119
Saul, King 20
Segal, Zindel 108–9
self-criticism 128–30
Shaitan 119
Solomon, King 19
sources of depression 35–7
step changes 46–51
Sumedho, Ajahn 56
symbols of melancholy 20–4

tathata 124
Tea Meditation 80
Teasdale, John 108–9
training 134

Va 77
values, personal 58–9, 61–3
vicious cycles 43, 65–6
   breaking free from 45–50
'vulnerability to depression' 38

white holes 25–7
Williams, Mark 108–9
wormholes 25–7

Zola, Émile 19

Acknowledgements

I would like to thank Martine Batchelor and Bhante Bodhidhamma for their contributions to this book.

I would also like to acknowledge the following people: Jon Kabat-Zinn for his pioneering efforts in bringing mindfulness into secular settings; Zindel Segal, Mark Williams and John Teasdale for their work on Mindfulness-Based Cognitive Therapy; Steven Hayes and Russ Harris for their work on values from the Acceptance and Commitment Therapy model; Peter Harvey for his astute guidance in the study of Buddhism; the teachers, writers, thinkers, scientists and therapists quoted within these pages.

More generally, I am indebted to the Gestalt Therapy tradition for its abiding emphasis on experiential awareness, and the Psychodynamic and Cognitive-Behavioural traditions for their formulations of depression.

Finally, I would like to express my enduring gratitude to the teachers and fellow practitioners from the Buddhist tradition with whom I have practised over the years. Without those who walk the ancient path, there would be no tracks to be found today.

About the Author

Richard Gilpin is a cognitive behavioural psychotherapist, counsellor and meditation instructor. He has trained extensively in mindfulness-based practices since the 1990s. He has an MA in Buddhist Studies and is co-founder of the Bodhi Garden, a UK registered charitable trust. His research into the origins and practices of Mindfulness-Based Cognitive Therapy was published in 2008. He is the author of *Find Your Path through Anxiety: Mindful techniques to help you find ease* (2025) and *Find Your Path through Depression: Mindful techniques for dark times* (2025). His website is www.richardgilpin.co.uk.

The *Find Your Path* Series

Find Your Path books shed light on a range of common mental-health struggles, from depression to imposter syndrome, and offer powerful techniques for navigating life's inevitable ups and downs.

Find Your Path through Anxiety: Mindful techniques to help you find ease (2025)

Find Your Path through Imposter Syndrome: Powerful techniques to help you see your worth (2025)